GREATEST EVER
Chocolate

p

This is a Parragon Publishing Book
This edition published in 2003

Parragon Publishing
Queen Street House
4 Queen Street
Bath BA1 1HE, UK

ISBN: 0-75259-947-X

Printed in Dubai

Produced by The Bridgewater Book Company Ltd

NOTE

Cup measurements in this book are for American cups. This book also uses
imperial and metric measurements. Follow the same units of measurement
throughout; do not mix imperial and metric.
All spoon measurements are level: teaspoons are assumed to be 5 ml and
tablespoons are assumed to be 15 ml. Unless otherwise stated, milk is assumed
to be whole milk, eggs and individual vegetables such as potatoes are medium,
and pepper is freshly ground black pepper.

The times given for each recipe are an approximate guide only because the
preparation times may differ according to the techniques used by different
people and the cooking times may vary as a result of the type of oven used.

Recipes using raw or very lightly cooked eggs should be
avoided by infants, the elderly, pregnant women, convalescents, and anyone
suffering from an illness.

Contents

Introduction

Chocolate! The mere mention of anything associated with this mouthwatering confection can cause a dreamy look to come into the eyes of the chocoholic.

The cocoa tree, Theobroma cacao, originated in South America, and from the early 7th century it was cultivated by the Maya, who established a flourishing trade and even used the cocoa bean as currency. In 1502, Christopher Columbus took the cocoa bean to Spain, but it wasn't until later that Cortés introduced xocotlatl, a recipe brought from the Mexican court of Montezuma for a drink made from crushed roasted cocoa beans and cold water. Vanilla, spices, honey, and sugar were added to improve the flavor of this thick and bitter brew, and over time it came to be served hot.

In the 17th century, the popularity of cocoa spread to the rest of Europe. France was the first country to fall to its charms, then Holland, where Amsterdam became the most important cocoa port beyond Spain. From there cocoa went to Germany, then north to Scandinavia, and also south to Italy. Cocoa arrived in England in the mid-17th century, and in London chocolate houses quickly began to rival the newly established coffee houses.

In the early 19th century, Dutch chemist Coenraad Van Houten invented a press to extract the fat from the beans, and developed a method of neutralizing the acids. In this way, he was able to produce almost pure cocoa butter, and a hard "cake," which could be milled to a powder for use as a flavoring. As a result, it became possible to eat chocolate as well as to drink it.

In Britain, Fry's chocolate appeared in 1847, and in Switzerland the famous chocolate companies were established. In 1875 chocolate was combined with condensed milk to produce the first milk chocolate. At around this time, Lindt found a way of making the smooth, melting chocolate still associated with his company today. About 20 years later, Hershey introduced his famous chocolate bar in the United States.

Cocoa trees are now grown in many parts of the world. The cocoa beans are left in the sun, then shelled, and the kernels processed to produce cocoa solids. Finally, the cocoa butter is extracted and further processed to become chocolate, in all its many guises.

Basic Recipes

Preparing Chocolate

To melt chocolate on a stove:

1 Break the chocolate into small, equal-size pieces and put it into a heatproof bowl.

2 Place the bowl over a pan of hot, simmering water, making sure the base of the bowl does not come into contact with the water.

3 Once the chocolate starts to melt, stir gently until smooth, then remove from the heat.

Note: Do not melt chocolate over direct heat (unless melting with other ingredients—in this case, keep the heat very low).

To melt chocolate in a microwave oven:

1 Break the chocolate into small pieces and place in a microwave-proof bowl.

2 Put the bowl in the microwave oven and melt. As a guide, melt 4½ oz/125 g semisweet chocolate on High for 2 minutes, and white or milk chocolate on Medium for 2–3 minutes.

Note: As microwave oven temperatures and settings vary, you should consult the manufacturer's instructions first.

3 Stir the chocolate, let stand for a few minutes, then stir again. If necessary, return it to the microwave for another 30 seconds.

Chocolate Decorations

Decorations add a special touch to a cake or pudding. They can be interleaved with non-stick baking parchment and stored in airtight containers. Semisweet chocolate will keep for 4 weeks, and milk or white chocolate for 2 weeks.

Caraque

1 Spread the melted chocolate over a clean acrylic cutting board and let it set.

2 When the chocolate has set, hold the board firmly, position a large, smooth-bladed knife on the chocolate, and pull the blade toward you at an angle of 45°, scraping along the chocolate to form the caraque. You should end up with irregularly shaped long curls.

3 Using the knife blade, lift the caraque off the board.

Quick Curls

1 For quick curls, choose a thick bar of chocolate, and keep it at room temperature.

2 Using a sharp, swivel-bladed vegetable peeler, scrape lightly along the chocolate to form fine curls, or more firmly to form thicker curls.

Note: Before grating chocolate, make sure the chocolate is firm. In warm weather, chill the chocolate in the refrigerator before using.

Leaves

1 Use freshly picked leaves with well-defined veins that are clean, dry, and pliable. Holding a leaf by its stem, paint a smooth layer of melted chocolate onto the underside with a small paint brush or pastry brush.

2 Repeat with the remaining leaves, then place them, chocolate-side up, on a baking sheet lined with waxed paper.

3 Let chill for at least 1 hour until set. When set, peel each leaf away from its chocolate coating.

Cakes, Gâteaux & Loaves

It is hard to resist the pleasure of a sumptuous

piece of chocolate cake and no chocolate book

would be complete without a selection of

cakes, gâteaux, and loaves—there are plenty to choose from in this chapter.

The more experimental among you can vary the fillings of decoration

according to what takes your fancy. Alternatively, follow our easy step-by-step

instructions and look at our glossy pictures to guide you to perfect results.

The gâteaux in this book are a feast for the eyes, and so are the delicious

cakes, many of which can be made with surprising ease. The loaves are the

perfect indulgence to enjoy with coffee and can be made with very little effort.

So next time you feel like a mouthwatering slice of something, these recipes

are sure to be a success.

chocolate almond cake

serves eight

6 oz/175 g semisweet chocolate

¾ cup butter

½ cup superfine sugar

4 eggs, separated

¼ tsp cream of tartar

⅓ cup self-rising flour

1¼ cups ground almonds

1 tsp almond extract

TOPPING

4½ oz/125 g light chocolate

2 tbsp butter

4 tbsp heavy cream

TO DECORATE

2 tbsp toasted slivered almonds

1 oz/25 g semisweet chocolate, melted

1 Lightly grease and line the bottom of a 9-inch/23-cm round springform pan. Break the chocolate into small pieces and place in a small pan with the butter. Heat gently, stirring until melted and well combined.

2 Place ½ cup of the superfine sugar in a bowl with the egg yolks and whisk until pale and creamy. Add the melted chocolate and butter mixture, beating until well combined.

3 Sift the cream of tartar and flour together and fold into the chocolate mixture with the ground almonds and almond extract.

4 Whisk the egg whites in a bowl until standing in soft peaks. Add the remaining superfine sugar and whisk for about 2 minutes by hand, or 45–60 seconds if using an electric mixer, until thick and glossy. Fold the

egg whites into the chocolate mixture and spoon into the prepared pan. Bake in a preheated oven, 375°F/190°C, for 40 minutes, until just springy to the touch. Let cool.

5 Heat the topping ingredients in a bowl over a pan of hot water. Remove from the heat and beat for 2 minutes. Let chill for 30 minutes. Transfer the cake to a plate and spread with the topping. Sprinkle with the slivered almonds and drizzle with melted chocolate. Let the topping set for 2 hours before serving.

chocolate tray bake

serves fifteen

3 cups self-rising flour, sifted

3 tbsp unsweetened cocoa, sifted

1 cup superfine sugar

1 cup soft margarine

4 eggs, beaten

4 tbsp milk

⅓ cup light chocolate chips

⅓ cup semisweet chocolate chips

⅓ cup white chocolate chips

confectioners' sugar, for dusting

VARIATION

For an attractive finish, cut thin strips of paper and lay in a criss-cross pattern on top of the cake. Dust with confectioners' sugar, then remove the paper strips.

1 Grease a 13 x 9 x 2-inch/ 33 x 23 x 5-cm cake pan with a little butter or margarine.

2 Place all of the ingredients except for the chocolate chips and confectioners' sugar in a large mixing bowl and beat together until smooth.

3 Beat in the light, semisweet, and white chocolate chips.

4 Spoon the mixture into the prepared cake pan and smooth the top. Bake in a preheated oven, 350°F/180°C, for 30–40 minutes, until risen and springy to the touch. Let cool in the pan.

5 Once cool, dust with confectioners' sugar. Cut into squares to serve.

chocolate & pineapple cake

serves nine

⅔ cup lowfat spread

½ cup superfine sugar

¾ cup self-rising flour, sifted

3 tbsp unsweetened cocoa, sifted

1½ tsp baking powder

2 eggs

8 oz/225 g canned unsweetened
pineapple pieces in fruit juice

½ cup lowfat thick plain yogurt

about 1 tbsp confectioners' sugar

grated chocolate, to decorate

COOK'S TIP

Store the cake, undecorated,
in an airtight container for
up to 3 days. Once decorated,
refrigerate and use within
2 days.

1 Lightly grease an 8-inch/20-cm square cake pan.

2 Place the lowfat spread, superfine sugar, flour, unsweetened cocoa, baking powder, and eggs in a large mixing bowl. Beat with a wooden spoon or electric mixer until smooth.

3 Pour the cake mixture into the prepared pan and smooth the surface. Bake in a preheated oven, 325°F/190°C, for 20–25 minutes or until springy to the touch. Let the chocolate and pineapple cake cool slightly in the pan before transferring to a wire rack to cool completely.

4 Drain the pineapple, chop the pineapple pieces, and drain again. Set aside a little pineapple for decoration, then stir the rest of the pineapple into the yogurt and sweeten to taste with confectioners' sugar.

5 Using a spatula, spread the pineapple and yogurt mixture smoothly and evenly over the top of the cake and decorate with the reserved pineapple pieces. Sprinkle with the grated chocolate.

family chocolate cake

serves eight

½ cup soft margarine

½ cup superfine sugar

2 eggs

1 tbsp light corn syrup

1 cup self-rising flour, sifted

2 tbsp unsweetened cocoa, sifted

FILLING AND TOPPING

4 tbsp confectioners' sugar, sifted

2 tbsp butter

3½ oz/100 g white or light cooking
chocolate

a little light or white chocolate,
melted (optional)

1 Lightly grease two 7-inch/18-cm shallow cake pans.

2 Place all of the ingredients for the cake in a large mixing bowl and beat with a wooden spoon or electric mixer to form a smooth mixture.

3 Divide the mixture between the prepared pans and smooth the tops. Bake in a preheated oven, 375°F/190°C, for 20 minutes or until springy to the touch. Cool for a few minutes in the pans before transferring to a wire rack to cool completely.

4 To make the filling, beat the confectioners' sugar and butter together in a bowl until light and fluffy. Melt the white or light cooking chocolate and beat half into the icing mixture. Use the filling to sandwich the 2 cakes together.

5 Spread the remaining melted cooking chocolate over the top of the cake. Pipe circles of contrasting melted light or white chocolate and feather into the cooking chocolate with a toothpick, if desired. Let the cake set before serving.

chocolate & orange cake

serves eight

¾ cup superfine sugar

¾ cup butter or block margarine

3 eggs, beaten

1½ cups self-rising flour, sifted

2 tbsp unsweetened cocoa, sifted

2 tbsp milk

3 tbsp orange juice

grated rind of ½ orange

FROSTING

1½ cups confectioners' sugar

2 tbsp orange juice

a little melted chocolate

VARIATION

Add 2 tablespoons of rum or brandy to the chocolate mixture instead of the milk. The cake also works well when flavored with grated lemon rind and juice instead of the orange.

1 Lightly grease an 8-inch/20-cm deep round cake pan.

2 Beat the sugar and butter or margarine together in a bowl until light and fluffy. Gradually add the eggs, beating well after each addition. Carefully fold in the flour.

3 Divide the mixture in half. Add the unsweetened cocoa and milk to one half, stirring until well combined. Flavor the other half with the orange juice and grated orange rind.

4 Place spoonfuls of each mixture into the prepared pan and swirl together with a skewer, to create a marbled effect. Bake in a preheated oven, 375°F/190°C, for 25 minutes or until the cake is springy to the touch.

5 Let the cake cool in the pan for a few minutes before transferring to a wire rack to cool completely.

6 To make the frosting, sift the confectioner's sugar into a mixing bowl and mix in enough of the orange juice to form a smooth frosting. Spread the frosting over the top of the cake and leave to set. Pipe fine lines of melted chocolate in a decorated pattern over the top.

mocha layer cake

serves eight

1¾ cups self-rising flour

¼ tsp baking powder

4 tbsp unsweetened cocoa

½ cup superfine sugar

2 eggs

2 tbsp light corn syrup

⅔ cup corn oil

⅔ cup milk

FILLING

1 tsp instant coffee powder

1 tbsp boiling water

1¼ cups heavy cream

2 tbsp confectioners' sugar

TO DECORATE

1¾ oz/50 g flock chocolate

chocolate caraque (see page 7)

confectioners' sugar, for dusting

1 Lightly grease three 7-inch/18-cm cake pans with butter.

2 Sift the flour, baking powder, and cocoa into a large mixing bowl. Stir in the sugar. Make a well in the center and stir in the eggs, syrup, oil, and milk. Beat with a wooden spoon, gradually mixing in the dry ingredients to make a smooth batter. Divide the cake mixture between the prepared pans.

3 Bake in a preheated oven, 350°F/180°C, for 35–45 minutes or until springy to the touch. Let cool in the pans for 5 minutes, then turn out onto a wire rack to cool completely.

4 Dissolve the instant coffee in the boiling water and place in a bowl with the cream and confectioners' sugar. Whip until the cream is just holding its shape. Use half of the cream to sandwich the 3 cakes together. Spread the remaining cream over the top and sides of the cake. Lightly press the flock chocolate into the cream around the edge of the cake.

5 Transfer to a serving plate. Lay the caraque over the top of the cake. Cut a few thin strips of baking parchment and place on top of the caraque. Dust lightly with confectioners' sugar, then carefully remove the paper. Serve.

devil's food cake

serves six

3½ oz/100 g semisweet chocolate

2¼ cups self-rising flour

1 tsp baking soda

1 cup butter

2⅔ cups dark brown sugar

1 tsp vanilla extract

3 eggs

½ cup buttermilk

scant 1 cup boiling water

FROSTING

1¼ cups superfine sugar

2 egg whites

1 tbsp lemon juice

3 tbsp orange juice

candied orange peel, to decorate

COOK'S TIP

If you prefer, use vanilla butter frosting to decorate the cake. Cream ¾ cup of butter until soft, then add 3 cups sifted confectioner's sugar and mix together. Stir in vanilla extract to taste. Alternatively, use whipped cream and store in the refrigerator.

1 Lightly grease two 8-inch/20-cm shallow round cake pans and line the bottoms with baking parchment. Melt the chocolate in a pan. Sift the flour and baking soda together.

2 Beat the butter and sugar in a bowl until pale and fluffy. Beat in the vanilla extract and the eggs one at a time, beating well after each addition. Add a little flour if the mixture starts to curdle.

3 Fold the melted semisweet chocolate into the mixture until well blended. Gradually fold in the remaining flour, then gently stir in the buttermilk and boiling water.

4 Divide the mixture between the pans and smooth the tops. Bake in a preheated oven, 375°F/190°C, for 30 minutes, until springy to the touch. Let the cake cool in the pan for 5 minutes, then transfer to a wire rack to cool completely.

5 Place the frosting ingredients in a large bowl set over a pan of gently simmering water. Whisk, preferably with an electric mixer, until thickened and forming soft peaks. Remove from the heat and whisk until the mixture is cool.

6 Sandwich the 2 cakes together with a little of the frosting, then, using a spatula, spread the remainder over the sides and top of the cake, swirling it as you do so. Decorate the top of the cake with the candied orange peel.

chocolate tea bread

serves four

¾ cup butter, softened

⅔ cup light brown sugar

4 eggs, beaten lightly

8 oz/225 g semisweet chocolate
   chips

½ cup raisins

½ cup chopped walnuts

finely grated rind of 1 orange

2 cups self-rising flour

1 Lightly grease a 2-lb/900-g loaf pan and line the bottom with baking parchment.

2 Cream the butter and light brown sugar together in a bowl until they are light and fluffy.

3 Gradually add the eggs, beating well after each addition. If the mixture starts to curdle, beat in 1–2 tablespoons of the flour.

4 Stir in the chocolate chips, raisins, walnuts, and orange rind. Sift the self-rising flour and carefully fold it into the mixture.

5 Spoon the mixture into the prepared loaf pan and then make a slight dip in the center of the top with the back of a spoon.

6 Bake in a preheated oven, 325°F/160°C, for 1 hour or until a fine skewer inserted into the center of the loaf comes out clean.

7 Let the loaf cool in the pan for 5 minutes before carefully turning out on to a wire rack. Let the loaf cool completely.

8 To serve the tea bread, cut it into thin slices.

rich chocolate layer cake

serves ten

7 eggs

scant 1 cup superfine sugar

1¼ cups all-purpose flour

½ cup unsweetened cocoa

4 tbsp butter, melted

FILLING

7 oz/200 g semisweet chocolate

½ cup butter

¼ cup confectioners' sugar

TO DECORATE

¾ cup lightly crushed, toasted
slivered almonds

quick chocolate curls (see page 7) or
grated chocolate

1 Grease a deep 9-inch/23-cm square cake pan and line the bottom with baking parchment.

2 Whisk the eggs and superfine sugar in a mixing bowl with an electric mixer for about 10 minutes or until the mixture is very light and foamy and the whisk leaves a trail that lasts a few seconds when lifted.

3 Sift the flour and cocoa together and fold half into the mixture. Drizzle over the melted butter and fold in the rest of the flour and cocoa. Pour into the prepared pan and bake in a preheated oven, 350°F/180°C, for 30–35 minutes or until springy to the touch. Let the cake cool slightly, then remove from the pan and cool completely on a wire rack. Wash and dry the pan and return the cake to it.

4 While the cake is cooling, make the filling. Melt the semisweet chocolate and butter together, then remove from the heat. Stir in the confectioners' sugar, let cool, then beat the filling until it is thick enough to spread.

5 Halve the cooled cake lengthwise and cut each half into 3 layers. Sandwich the layers together with three-quarters of the chocolate filling. Spread the remainder over the cake and mark a wavy pattern on the top. Press the almonds onto the sides. Decorate the cake with chocolate curls or grated chocolate.

chocolate passion cake

serves six

5 eggs

⅔ cup superfine sugar

1¼ cups all-purpose flour

⅓ cup unsweetened cocoa

2 carrots, peeled, grated finely,
    and squeezed until dry

⅓ cup chopped walnuts

2 tbsp corn oil

12 oz/350 g medium-fat soft cheese

1½ cups confectioners' sugar

6 oz/175 g light or semisweet
    chocolate, melted

1 Lightly grease and line the bottom of a 8-inch/20-cm deep round cake pan with baking parchment.

2 Place the eggs and sugar in a large mixing bowl set over a pan of gently simmering water and whisk until the mixture is thick enough to leave a trail.

3 Remove the bowl from the heat. Sift the flour and cocoa into the bowl and carefully fold in. Fold in the grated carrots, walnuts, and oil.

4 Pour into the prepared pan and bake in a preheated oven, 375°F/190°C, for 45 minutes. Turn out onto a wire rack to cool.

5 Beat the soft cheese and confectioners' sugar together until combined. Beat in the melted chocolate. Split the cake in half and sandwich together again with half of the chocolate mixture. Cover the top of the cake with the remainder of the chocolate mixture, swirling it with a knife. Let chill, or serve immediately.

chocolate yogurt cake

serves eight

⅔ cup vegetable oil

⅔ cup whole-milk plain yogurt

1¼ cups brown sugar

3 eggs, beaten

¾ cup whole-wheat self-rising flour

1 cup self-rising flour, sifted

2 tbsp unsweetened cocoa

1 tsp baking soda

1¾ oz/50 g semisweet chocolate, melted

FILLING AND TOPPING

⅔ cup whole-milk plain yogurt

⅔ cup heavy cream

8 oz/225 g fresh soft fruit, such as strawberries or raspberries

1 Grease a 9-inch/23-cm round deep cake pan and line the bottom with baking parchment.

2 Place the oil, yogurt, sugar, and beaten eggs in a large mixing bowl and beat together until well combined. Sift the flours, cocoa, and baking soda together and beat into the bowl until well combined. Beat in the melted semisweet chocolate.

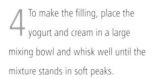

3 Pour the mixture into the prepared pan and bake in a preheated oven, 350°F/180°C, for 45–50 minutes or until a fine skewer inserted into the center comes out clean. Let the cake cool in the pan for 5 minutes, then turn out onto a wire rack to cool completely. When cold, split the cake into 3 layers.

4 To make the filling, place the yogurt and cream in a large mixing bowl and whisk well until the mixture stands in soft peaks.

5 Place one layer of cake onto a serving plate and spread with some of the cream. Top with a little of the fruit (slicing larger fruit such as strawberries). Repeat with the next layer. Top with the final layer of cake and spread with the rest of the cream. Arrange more fruit on top and cut the cake into wedges to serve.

raspberry vacherin

serves ten

3 egg whites

¾ cup superfine sugar

1 tsp cornstarch

1 oz/25 g semisweet chocolate, grated

FILLING

6 oz/175 g semisweet chocolate

2 cups heavy cream, whipped

12 oz/350 g fresh raspberries

a little melted chocolate, to decorate

COOK'S TIP

When whisking egg whites, make sure your bowl is spotlessly clean and free from any grease as the egg whites will not whisk well or hold their shape.

1 Draw 3 rectangles, 4 x 10 inches/ 10 x 25 cm, on sheets of baking parchment, and place on 2 cookie sheets.

2 Whisk the egg whites in a mixing bowl until standing in soft peaks, then gradually whisk in half of the sugar and continue whisking until the mixture is very stiff and glossy.

3 Carefully fold in the rest of the superfine sugar, the cornstarch, and the grated chocolate with a metal spoon or spatula.

4 Spoon the meringue mixture into a pastry bag fitted with a ½-inch/1-cm plain tip and pipe lines across the rectangles.

5 Bake the meringues in a preheated oven, 275°F/140°C, for 1½ hours, changing the positions of

the cookie sheets halfway through. Without opening the oven door, turn off the oven and let the meringues cool inside the oven, then carefully peel away the baking parchment.

6 To make the filling, melt the chocolate and spread it over 2 of the meringues. Let harden.

7 Place 1 chocolate-coated meringue on a plate and top with about one-third of the cream and raspberries. Gently place the second chocolate-coated meringue on top and spread with half of the remaining cream and raspberries.

8 Place the last meringue on the top and decorate with the remaining cream and raspberries. Drizzle a little melted chocolate over the top and serve.

sachertorte

serves ten

6 oz/175 g semisweet chocolate

⅔ cup unsalted butter

⅔ cup superfine sugar

6 eggs, separated

1¼ cups all-purpose flour

FROSTING AND FILLING

6 oz/175 g semisweet chocolate

5 tbsp strong black coffee

1 cup frosting confectioners' sugar

6 tbsp good-quality apricot jelly

1¾ oz/50 g semisweet chocolate,
    melted, to decorate

COOK'S TIP

The finished cake is delicious
served with whipped cream
and fresh raspberries or a
raspberry coulis.

1 Grease a 9-inch/23-cm springform cake pan and line the bottom with baking parchment. Melt the chocolate. Beat the butter and ⅓ cup of the sugar until pale and fluffy. Add the egg yolks and beat well. Add the chocolate in a thin stream, beating well. Sift the flour and fold it into the mixture. Whisk the egg whites until standing in soft peaks. Add the remaining sugar and whisk for 2 minutes by hand, or 45–60 seconds if using an electric mixer, until glossy. Fold half into the chocolate mixture, then fold in the remainder.

2 Spoon into the prepared pan and smooth the top. Bake in a preheated oven, 300°F/150°C, for 1–1¼ hours until a skewer inserted into the center comes out clean. Cool in the pan for 5 minutes, then transfer to a wire rack and let cool completely.

3 To make the frosting, melt the chocolate and beat in the coffee until smooth. Strain the confectioners' sugar into a bowl. Whisk in the melted chocolate mixture to give a thick frosting. Halve the cake. Warm the apricot jelly, spread over one half of the cake and sandwich together. Invert the cake onto a wire rack. Spoon the frosting over the cake and, using a spatula, spread as smoothly and evenly as possible, to coat the top and sides. Let the frosting set for 5 minutes, allowing any excess to drip through the rack. Transfer to a serving plate and let set for at least 2 hours.

4 To decorate, spoon the melted chocolate into a small pastry bag and pipe the word "Sacher" or "Sachertorte" on the top of the cake. Let it harden before serving the cake.

chocolate marshmallow cake

serves six

6 tbsp unsalted butter

generous 1 cup superfine sugar

½ tsp vanilla extract

2 eggs, beaten lightly

3 oz/85 g semisweet chocolate,
   broken into pieces

⅔ cup buttermilk

1¼ cups self-rising flour

½ tsp baking soda

pinch of salt

2 oz/55 g light chocolate, grated,
   to decorate

FROSTING

6 oz/175 g white marshmallows

1 tbsp milk

2 egg whites

2 tbsp superfine sugar

1 Grease a 3¾-cup ovenproof bowl with butter. Cream the butter, sugar, and vanilla together in a bowl until pale and fluffy, then gradually beat in the eggs.

2 Melt the semisweet chocolate in a heatproof bowl over a pan of simmering water. When the chocolate has melted, stir in the buttermilk gradually, until well combined. Remove the pan from the heat and cool slightly.

3 Sift the flour, baking soda, and salt into a separate bowl.

4 Add the chocolate mixture and the flour mixture alternately to the creamed mixture, a little at a time. Spoon the mixture into the ovenproof bowl and smooth the surface.

5 Bake in a preheated oven, 325°F/160°C, for 50 minutes until a skewer inserted into the center of the cake comes out clean. Turn out onto a wire rack to cool.

6 Meanwhile, make the frosting. Put the marshmallows and milk in a small pan and heat very gently until the marshmallows have melted. Remove the pan from the heat and set aside to cool.

7 Whisk the egg whites until soft peaks form, then add the sugar and continue whisking, until stiff peaks form. Fold the egg white into the cooled marshmallow mixture and set aside for 10 minutes.

8 When the cake is cool, cover the top and sides with the marshmallow frosting. Top with grated light chocolate.

chocolate slab cake

serves ten

1 cup butter

3½ oz/100 g semisweet chocolate,
    chopped

⅔ cup water

2½ cups all-purpose flour

2 tsp baking powder

1⅔ cups soft brown sugar

⅔ cup sour cream

2 eggs, beaten

FROSTING

7 oz/200 g semisweet chocolate

6 tbsp water

3 tbsp light cream

1 tbsp butter, chilled

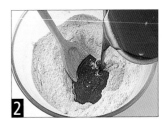

1 Grease a 13 x 8-inch/33 x 20-cm square cake pan and line the bottom with baking parchment. In a pan, melt the butter and chocolate with the water over low heat, stirring frequently.

2 Sift the flour and baking powder into a mixing bowl and stir in the sugar. Pour the hot chocolate liquid into the bowl.

3 Beat well until all of the ingredients are evenly mixed. Stir in the sour cream, followed by the beaten eggs and mix well.

4 Pour the mixture into the prepared pan and bake in a preheated oven, 375°F/190°C, for 40–45 minutes.

5 Let the cake cool in the pan before turning it out onto a wire rack to cool completely.

6 To make the frosting, melt the chocolate with the water in a pan over very low heat, stir in the cream and remove from the heat. Stir in the chilled butter, then pour the frosting over the cooled cake, using a spatula to spread it evenly over the top of the cake.

COOK'S TIP

Frost the cake while it is still on the wire rack, and place a large cookie sheet underneath to catch any drips. Spoon any drips back onto the cake.

mousse cake

serves twelve

¾ cup butter

¾ cup superfine sugar

4 eggs, beaten lightly

1 tbsp unsweetened cocoa

1¾ cups self-rising flour

1¾ oz/50 g semisweet, orange-
flavored chocolate, melted

ORANGE MOUSSE

2 eggs, separated

4 tbsp superfine sugar

generous ¾ cup freshly squeezed
orange juice

2 tsp powdered gelatin

3 tbsp water

1¼ cups heavy cream

peeled orange slices, to decorate

1 Grease an 8-inch/20-cm
springform cake pan and line the
bottom with baking parchment. Beat
the butter and sugar together in a
bowl until light and fluffy. Gradually
add the eggs, beating well after each
addition. Sift the cocoa and flour
together and fold into the cake
mixture. Fold in the melted chocolate.

2 Pour into the prepared pan and
smooth the top. Bake in a
preheated oven, 350°F/180°C, for 40
minutes or until springy to the touch.
Let the cake cool for 5 minutes in the
pan, then turn out and cool completely.

3 Meanwhile, make the orange
mousse. Beat the egg yolks and
sugar until light, then whisk in the
orange juice. Sprinkle the gelatin over
the water in a small bowl and let it go
spongy, then place over a pan of hot
water and stir until the gelatin has
dissolved. Stir into the mousse.

4 Whip the cream until holding
its shape, set aside a little for
decoration, and fold the rest into the
mousse. Whisk the egg whites until
standing in soft peaks, then fold in.
Let stand in a cool place until starting
to set, stirring occasionally.

5 Cut the cold cake into 2 layers.
Place half of the cake in the pan.
Pour in the mousse and press the
second cake layer on top. Chill until
set. Transfer to a plate, pipe cream
rosettes on the top, and arrange
orange slices in the center.

chocolate roulade

serves six

5½ oz/150 g semisweet chocolate

2 tbsp water

6 eggs

¾ cup superfine sugar

¼ cup all-purpose flour

1 tbsp unsweetened cocoa

FILLING

1¼ cups heavy cream

2¾ oz/75 g sliced strawberries

TO DECORATE

confectioners' sugar, for dusting

chocolate leaves (see page 7)

fresh strawberries, to serve

1 Line a 15 x 10-inch/38 x 25-cm jelly roll pan. Melt the chocolate in the water, stirring. Let cool slightly.

2 Place the eggs and sugar in a bowl and whisk for 10 minutes or until the mixture is pale and foamy and the whisk leaves a trail when lifted. Whisk in the chocolate in a thin stream. Sift the flour and cocoa together and fold into the mixture. Pour into the pan and smooth the top.

3 Bake in a preheated oven, 400°F/200°C, for 12 minutes. Dust a sheet of baking parchment with a little confectioners' sugar. Turn out the roulade and remove the lining paper. Roll up the roulade with the fresh parchment inside. Place on a wire rack, cover with a damp dish towel, and let cool.

4 Whisk the cream. Unroll the roulade and sprinkle over the fruit. Spread three-quarters of the cream over the roulade and re-roll. Dust with confectioners' sugar.

5 Place the roulade on a plate. Pipe the rest of the cream down the center. Make the chocolate leaves and use to decorate the roulade. Serve with strawberries.

chocolate & coconut roulade

serves eight

3 eggs

⅓ cup superfine sugar

⅓ cup self-rising flour

1 tbsp block creamed coconut,
softened with 1 tbsp boiling
water

¼ cup shredded coconut

6 tbsp good-quality raspberry jelly

CHOCOLATE COATING

7 oz/200 g semisweet chocolate

5 tbsp butter

2 tbsp light corn syrup

RASPBERRY COULIS

8 oz/225 g fresh or frozen
raspberries, thawed if frozen

2 tbsp water

4 tbsp confectioners' sugar

1 Grease and line a 9 x 12-inch/
23 x 30-cm jelly roll pan. Whisk
the eggs and superfine sugar in a large
mixing bowl with an electric mixer for
about 10 minutes or until the mixture
is very light and foamy and the whisk
leaves a trail that lasts a few seconds
when lifted.

2 Sift the flour and fold in with a
metal spoon or spatula. Fold in
the creamed coconut and shredded
coconut. Pour into the prepared pan
and bake in a preheated oven,
400°F/200°C, for 10–12 minutes
or until springy to the touch.

3 Sprinkle a sheet of baking
parchment with a little superfine
sugar and place on top of a damp dish
towel. Turn the cake out onto the
paper and carefully peel away the
lining parchment. Spread the raspberry
jelly over the sponge and roll up from
one of the short ends, using the dish
towel to help you. Place the roulade
seam-side down on a wire rack and let
cool completely.

4 Meanwhile, make the coating.
Melt the chocolate and butter,
stirring. Stir in the syrup and let the
mixture cool for 5 minutes. Spread it
over the roulade and let stand until set.

5 to make the coulis, blend the fruit
to a purée in a food processor
with the water and sugar, and strain to
remove the seeds. Cut the roulade into
slices and serve with the coulis and a
few fresh raspberries.

33

chocolate brownie roulade

serves eight

5 ½ oz/150 g semisweet chocolate,
   broken into pieces

3 tbsp water

¾ cup superfine sugar

5 eggs, separated

2 tbsp raisins, chopped

2 tbsp chopped pecans

pinch of salt

1 ¼ cups heavy cream, whipped
   lightly

confectioners' sugar, for dusting

1 Grease a 12 x 8-inch/30 x 20-cm
jelly roll pan, line with baking
parchment, and grease the parchment.

2 Melt the chocolate with the water
in a small pan over low heat until
the chocolate has just melted. Let the
chocolate cool.

3 Whisk the sugar and egg yolks In
a bowl for 2–3 minutes with
an electric mixer until thick and pale.

4 Fold in the cooled chocolate,
raisins, and pecans.

5 Whisk the egg whites In a
separate bowl with the salt. Fold
one-quarter of the egg whites into the
chocolate mixture, then fold in the rest
of the whites, working lightly and
quickly so as not to lose any air.

6 Transfer the mixture to the
prepared pan and bake in a
preheated oven, 350°F/180°C, for
25 minutes, until risen and just firm
to the touch. Let the cake cool before
covering with a sheet of non-stick
baking parchment and a damp clean
dish towel. Set aside until cold.

7 Turn the roulade out onto another
piece of baking parchment dusted
with confectioners' sugar and remove
the lining paper.

8 Spread the cream over the
roulade. Starting from a short
end, roll the roulade away from you
using the parchment to guide you. Trim
the ends of the roulade to make a neat
finish and transfer to a serving plate.
Chill in the refrigerator until ready to
serve. Dust with a little confectioners'
sugar before serving.

almond & hazelnut gâteau

serves eight

4 eggs

½ cup superfine sugar

½ cup ground almonds

½ cup ground hazelnuts

⅓ cup all-purpose flour

½ cup slivered almonds

FILLING

3½ oz/100 g semisweet chocolate

1 tbsp butter

1¼ cups heavy cream

confectioners' sugar, for dusting

1 Grease 2 round 7-inch/18-cm layer cake pans and line the bottoms with baking parchment.

2 Whisk the eggs and superfine sugar in a large mixing bowl with an electric mixer for about 10 minutes or until the mixture is very light and foamy and the whisk leaves a trail that lasts a few seconds when lifted.

3 Fold in the ground nuts, sift the flour and fold in with a metal spoon or spatula. Pour the mixture into the prepared pans.

4 Sprinkle the slivered almonds over the top of one of the cakes. Bake both of the cakes in a preheated oven, 375°F/190°C, for 15–20 minutes or until springy to the touch.

5 Let the cakes cool slightly in the pans. Carefully remove the cakes from the pans and transfer them to a wire rack to cool completely.

6 Meanwhile, make the filling. Melt the chocolate, remove from the heat, and stir in the butter. Let the mixture cool slightly. Whip the cream until just holding its shape, then fold in the melted chocolate until mixed.

7 Place the cake without the extra almonds on a serving plate and spread the filling over it. Let the filling set slightly, then place the almond-topped cake on top and let chill for about 1 hour. Dust the cake with confectioners' sugar and serve.

layered meringue gâteau

serves eight

6 egg whites

¾ cup superfine sugar

1½ cups confectioners' sugar

2 tbsp cornstarch

FILLING

1 cup heavy cream

5 oz/140 g semisweet chocolate

4 tsp dark rum

TO DECORATE

⅔ cup heavy cream

4 tsp superfine sugar

1–2 tsp unsweetened cocoa

1 Prepare 5 sheets of baking parchment by drawing a 7-inch/18-cm circle on each. Use them to line cookie sheets.

2 Whisk the egg whites until they form soft peaks. Mix together both sugars and cornstarch and strain it into the egg whites, a little at a time, whisking until firm peaks form.

3 Spoon the meringue mixture into a pastry bag fitted with a round tip. Starting from the center, carefully pipe 5 spirals, measuring 7 inches/ 18 cm, on each of the prepared pieces of baking parchment.

4 Bake in a preheated oven, at the lowest possible temperature with the oven door kept slightly ajar, for 6 hours or overnight.

5 After baking, carefully peel the meringue spirals from the parchment and cool on wire racks.

6 To make the filling, pour the cream into a pan and place over low heat. Break the chocolate into small pieces and add to the pan. Stir until melted. Remove from the heat and beat the mixture with a hand-held whisk. Beat in the rum, then cover with plastic wrap and chill overnight or for as long as the meringues are baking.

7 To assemble the gâteau, beat the filling with an electric mixer until thick and smooth. Place 3 of the meringue layers on a counter and spread the filling over them. Stack the 3 meringue layers, one on top of the other, and place an uncovered meringue layer on top. Crush the fifth meringue layer into crumbs.

8 To make the decoration, whip the cream with the sugar until thick. Carefully spread the cream mixture over the top of the gâteau. Sprinkle the meringue crumbs on top of the cream and dust the center of the gâteau with unsweetened cocoa. Serve within 1–2 hours.

chocolate & walnut cake

serves eight

4 eggs

½ cup superfine sugar

1 cup all-purpose flour

1 tbsp unsweetened cocoa

2 tbsp butter, melted

2¾ oz/75 g semisweet chocolate,
    melted

1¼ cups finely chopped walnuts

FROSTING

2¾ oz/75 g semisweet chocolate

½ cup butter

1¼ cups confectioners' sugar

2 tbsp milk

walnut halves, to decorate

1 Grease a deep 7-inch/18-cm round cake pan and line the bottom. Place the eggs and superfine sugar in a mixing bowl and beat with an electric mixer for 10 minutes or until the mixture is light and foamy and the whisk leaves a trail that lasts a few seconds when lifted.

2 Sift the flour together and cocoa and fold in with a metal spoon or spatula. Fold in the melted butter and chocolate, and the chopped walnuts. Pour into the prepared pan and bake in a preheated oven, 325°F/160°C, for 30–35 minutes or until the cake is springy to the touch.

3 Let the cake cool in the pan for 5 minutes, then transfer to a wire rack to cool completely.

4 Meanwhile, make the frosting. Melt the semisweet chocolate and let it cool slightly. Beat the butter, confectioners' sugar, and milk together in a bowl until pale and fluffy. Whisk in the melted chocolate.

5 Cut the cold cake into 2 layers. Sandwich the 2 layers with some of the frosting and place on a serving plate. Spread the remaining frosting over the top of the cake with a spatula, swirling it slightly as you do so. Decorate the finished cake with the walnut halves and serve.

dobos torte

serves eight

3 eggs

½ cup superfine sugar

1 tsp vanilla extract

¾ cup all-purpose flour

FILLING

6 oz/175 g semisweet chocolate

¾ cup butter

2 tbsp milk

3 cups confectioners' sugar

CARAMEL

½ cup granulated sugar

4 tbsp water

1 Draw four 7-inch/18-cm circles on sheets of baking parchment. Place 2 of them upside down on 2 cookie sheets.

2 Beat the eggs and superfine sugar in a large mixing bowl with an electric mixer for 10 minutes or until light and foamy. Fold in the vanilla extract. Sift the flour and fold in.

3 Spoon one-quarter of the mixture onto one of the cookie sheets and spread out to the size of the circle. Repeat with the other circle. Bake in a preheated oven, 400°F/200°C, for 5–8 minutes. Cool on wire racks. Repeat with the remaining mixture.

4 To make the filling, melt the chocolate and cool slightly. Beat the butter, milk, and confectioners' sugar together until pale and fluffy. Whisk in the melted chocolate.

5 Place the sugar and water for the caramel in a heavy-based pan. Heat gently, stirring, to dissolve the sugar. Boil gently until pale golden in color. Remove from the heat. Pour over one cake layer as a topping. Let harden slightly, then carefully mark into 8 portions with an oiled knife.

6 Remove the cakes from the parchment. Trim the edges. Sandwich the layers together with some of the filling, finishing with the caramel-topped cake. Spread the sides with the filling, and pipe rosettes around the top.

apricot & chocolate ring

serves twelve

⅓ cup diced butter

4 cups self-rising flour, sifted

4 tbsp superfine sugar

2 eggs, beaten

⅔ cup milk

FILLING AND DECORATION

2 tbsp butter, melted

5½ oz/150 g dried apricots, chopped

⅔ cup semisweet chocolate chips

1–2 tbsp milk, for glazeing

1 oz/25 g semisweet chocolate,
    melted

1 Grease a 10-inch/25-cm round cake pan and line the bottom with baking parchment.

2 Rub the butter into the flour until the mixture resembles fine bread crumbs. Stir in the superfine sugar, eggs, and milk to form a soft dough.

3 Roll out the dough on a lightly floured counter to form a 14-inch/35-cm square.

4 Brush the melted butter over the surface of the dough. Mix together the apricots and chocolate chips and, using a spoon or knife, spread them over the dough to within 1 inch/2.5 cm of the top and bottom.

5 Roll up the dough tightly, like a jelly roll, and cut it into 1-inch/2.5-cm slices. Stand the slices in a ring around the edge of the prepared pan at a slight tilt. Brush the surface with a little milk to glaze.

6 Bake in a preheated oven, 350°F/180°C, for 30 minutes or until cooked and golden. Let cool in the pan for about 15 minutes, then transfer to a wire rack to cool.

7 Drizzle the melted chocolate over the ring to decorate.

semisweet & white chocolate torte

serves six

4 eggs

½ cup superfine sugar

¾ cup all-purpose flour

DARK CHOCOLATE CREAM

⅔ cup heavy cream

5½ oz/150 g semisweet chocolate, broken into small pieces

WHITE CHOCOLATE FROSTING

2¾ oz/75 g white chocolate

1 tbsp butter

1 tbsp milk

4 tbsp confectioners' sugar

chocolate caraque (see page 7)

1 Grease an 8-inch/20-cm round springform cake pan and line the bottom. Beat the eggs and superfine sugar in a large mixing bowl with an electric mixer for about 10 minutes or until the mixture is very light and foamy and the whisk leaves a trail that lasts a few seconds when lifted.

2 Sift the flour and fold in with a metal spoon or spatula. Pour into the prepared pan and bake in a preheated oven, 350°F/180°C, for 35–40 minutes or until springy to the touch. Let the cake cool slightly, then transfer to a wire rack and let cool completely.

3 While the cake is cooling, make the chocolate cream. Place the cream in a pan and bring to a boil, stirring. Add the chocolate and stir until melted and well combined. Remove from the heat, transfer to a bowl, and let cool. Beat the chocolate cream with a wooden spoon until thick.

4 Cut the cold cake into 2 layers horizontally. Sandwich the layers back together with the chocolate cream and place on a wire rack.

5 To make the frosting, melt the chocolate and butter together and

stir until blended. Whisk in the milk and confectioners' sugar, and continue whisking until cool. Pour over the cake and spread with a spatula to coat the top and sides. Decorate with chocolate caraque and let the frosting set.

bistvitny torte

serves ten

CHOCOLATE TRIANGLES

1 oz/25 g semisweet chocolate, melted

1 oz/25 g white chocolate, melted

CAKE

¾ cup soft margarine

¾ cup superfine sugar

½ tsp vanilla extract

3 eggs, beaten lightly

2 cups self-rising flour

1¾ oz/50 g semisweet chocolate

SYRUP

½ cup granulated sugar

6 tbsp water

3 tbsp brandy or sherry

⅔ cup heavy cream

1 Grease a 9-inch/23-cm ring pan. To make the triangles, place a sheet of baking parchment onto a cookie sheet and place alternate spoonfuls of the semisweet and white chocolate onto the paper. Spread together to form a thick marbled layer, and let set. Cut into squares, then into triangles.

2 To make the cake, beat the margarine and sugar until light and fluffy. Beat in the vanilla extract. Gradually add the eggs, beating well. Fold in the flour. Divide the mixture in half. Melt the semisweet chocolate and stir into one half.

3 Place spoonfuls of each mixture into the prepared pan and swirl them together with a toothpick to create a marbled effect.

4 Bake in a preheated oven, 375°F/190°C, for 30 minutes or until the cake is springy to the touch. Let the cake cool in the pan for a few minutes, then transfer it to a wire rack and let cool completely.

5 To make the syrup, place the sugar in a small pan with the water and heat until the sugar has dissolved. Boil for 1–2 minutes. (Do not leave the pan unattended while the syrup is boiling.) Remove from the heat and stir in the brandy or sherry. Let the syrup cool slightly, then spoon it slowly all over the cake, letting it soak into the sponge. Whip the cream and pipe swirls of it on top of the cake. Decorate with the marbled chocolate triangles and serve.

chocolate & almond torte

serves ten

8 oz/225 g semisweet chocolate,
broken into pieces

3 tbsp water

1 cup brown sugar

¾ cup butter, softened

¼ cup ground almonds

3 tbsp self-rising flour

5 eggs, separated

⅔ cup finely chopped blanched
almonds

confectioners' sugar, for dusting

heavy cream, to serve

COOK'S TIP

For a nuttier flavor, toast
the chopped almonds in a
dry skillet over medium
heat for about 2 minutes
until lightly golden.

1 Grease a 9-inch/23-cm loose-bottomed cake pan and line the bottom with baking parchment.

2 Melt the chocolate with the water in a pan set over very low heat, stirring until smooth. Add the sugar and stir until dissolved, taking the pan off the heat to prevent it overheating.

3 Add the butter in small amounts until it has melted into the chocolate. Remove from the heat and lightly stir in the ground almonds and flour. Add the egg yolks one at a time, beating well after each addition.

4 Whisk the egg whites in a large mixing bowl, until they stand in soft peaks, then fold them into the chocolate mixture with a metal spoon. Stir in the chopped almonds. Pour the mixture into the prepared cake pan and smooth the surface.

5 Bake in a preheated oven, 350°F/180°C, for 40–45 minutes, until well risen and firm (the cake will crack on the surface during cooking).

6 Let cool in the pan for 30–40 minutes, then turn out onto a wire rack to cool completely. Dust with confectioners' sugar and serve in slices with cream.

date & chocolate cake

serves eight

4 oz/115 g semisweet chocolate,
  broken into pieces

1 tbsp grenadine

1 tbsp light corn syrup

½ cup unsalted butter, 2 tsp extra
  for greasing

4 tbsp superfine sugar

2 large eggs

⅔ cup self-rising flour

1 tbsp extra for dusting

2 tbsp ground rice

1 tbsp confectioners' sugar,
  to decorate

FILLING

⅔ cup chopped dried dates

1 tbsp lemon juice

1 tbsp orange juice

1 tbsp raw brown sugar

¼ cup chopped blanched almonds

2 tbsp apricot jelly

1 Grease and flour two 7-inch/18-cm layer cake pans. Put the chocolate, grenadine, and syrup in the top of a double boiler or in a heatproof bowl set over a pan of barely simmering water. Stir over low heat until the chocolate has melted and the mixture is smooth. Remove from the heat and let the mixture cool.

2 Cream the butter and superfine sugar together until pale and fluffy, then gradually beat in the eggs, then the cooled chocolate mixture.

3 Sift the flour into another bowl and stir in the ground rice. Carefully fold the flour mixture into the creamed mixture.

4 Divide the mixture between the prepared cake pans and smooth the surface with a spatula. Bake in a preheated oven, 350°F/180°C, for 20–25 minutes, until golden and firm to the touch. Turn the cakes out onto a wire rack to cool.

5 To make the filling, put all the ingredients into a pan and stir over low heat for 4–5 minutes, until fully incorporated. Remove from the heat, let cool, and then use the filling to sandwich the cakes together. Dust the top of the cake with confectioners' sugar to decorate.

white truffle cake

serves twelve

2 eggs

4 tbsp superfine sugar

⅓ cup all-purpose flour

1¾ oz/50 g white chocolate, melted

TRUFFLE TOPPING

1¼ cups heavy cream

12 oz/350 g white chocolate,
   broken into pieces

9 oz/250 g mascarpone cheese

TO DECORATE

semisweet, light, or white chocolate
   caraque (see page 7)

unsweetened cocoa, for dusting

1 Grease an 8-inch/20-cm round
  springform cake pan and line.

2 Whisk the eggs and superfine
  sugar in a mixing bowl for
10 minutes or until the mixture is very
light and foamy and the whisk leaves
a trail that lasts a few seconds when
lifted. Sift the flour and fold in with a
metal spoon. Fold in the melted white
chocolate. Pour into the pan and bake
in a preheated oven, 350°F/180°C,
for 25 minutes or until springy to the
touch. Let cool slightly, then transfer
to a wire rack until completely cold.
Return the cold cake to the pan.

3 To make the topping, place the
  cream in a pan and bring to a
boil, stirring to prevent it sticking to the
bottom of the pan. Cool slightly, then

add the white chocolate pieces and stir
until melted and combined. Remove
from the heat and stir until almost cool,
then stir in the mascarpone cheese.
Pour the mixture on top of the cake
and let chill for 2 hours.

4 Remove the cake from the pan
  and transfer to a plate. Make the
caraque (see page 7) and then use it to
decorate the top of the cake.

chocolate & vanilla loaf

serves ten

¾ cup superfine sugar

¾ cup soft margarine

½ tsp vanilla extract

3 eggs

2 cups self-rising flour, sifted

1¾ oz/50 g semisweet chocolate

confectioners' sugar, for dusting

COOK'S TIP

Freeze the loaf undecorated
for up to 2 months. Thaw at
room temperature.

1 Lightly grease a 1-lb/450-g loaf pan and set aside.

2 Beat the sugar and soft margarine together in a bowl until the mixture is light and fluffy.

3 Beat in the vanilla extract. Gradually add the eggs, beating well after each addition. Carefully fold the flour into the mixture.

4 Divide the mixture in half. Gently melt the semisweet chocolate and stir it carefully into one half of the mixture until well combined.

5 Place the vanilla mixture in the pan and smooth the top. Spread the chocolate layer over the vanilla layer.

6 Bake in a preheated oven, 375°F/190°C, for 30 minutes or until springy to the touch.

7 Let the loaf cool in the pan for a few minutes before transferring to a wire rack to cool completely.

8 Serve the loaf dusted with confectioners' sugar.

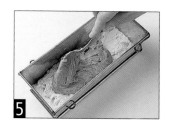

no-bake refrigerator cake

serves eight

1 cup unsalted butter, diced

8 oz/225 g semisweet chocolate, broken into pieces

⅓ cup chopped candied cherries

½ cup chopped walnuts

12 rectangular semisweet chocolate cookies

1 Line a 1-lb/450-g loaf pan with waxed paper or baking parchment. Set aside.

2 Put the butter and chocolate into the top of a double boiler or in a heatproof bowl set over a pan of barely simmering water. Stir constantly over low heat until they have melted and the mixture is smooth. Remove from the heat and cool slightly.

3 Mix the cherries and walnuts together in a bowl. Spoon one-third of the chocolate mixture into the prepared pan, cover with a layer of cookies, and top with half the cherries and walnuts. Make further layers, ending with the chocolate mixture. Cover with plastic wrap and let chill in the refrigerator for at least 12 hours. When thoroughly chilled, turn the cake out onto a serving dish.

chocolate ganache cake

serves ten

¾ cup butter

¾ cup superfine sugar

4 eggs, beaten lightly

1¾ cups self-rising flour

1 tbsp unsweetened cocoa

1¾ oz/50 g semisweet chocolate,
   melted

GANACHE

2 cups heavy cream

13 oz/375 g semisweet chocolate,
   broken into pieces

7 oz/200 g chocolate-flavored cake
   covering, to finish

1 Lightly grease an 8-inch/20-cm springform cake pan and line the bottom. Beat the butter and sugar until light and fluffy. Gradually add the eggs, beating well. Sift the flour and cocoa together. Fold into the cake mixture. Fold in the melted chocolate.

2 Pour into the prepared pan and smooth the top. Bake in a preheated oven, 350°F/180°C, for 40 minutes or until springy to the touch. Let cool for 5 minutes in the pan, then turn out onto a wire rack. Cut the cold cake into 2 layers.

3 To make the ganache, place the cream in a pan and bring to a boil, stirring. Add the chocolate and stir until melted and combined. Pour into a bowl and whisk for about 5 minutes or until the ganache is fluffy and cool.

4 Set aside one-third of the ganache. Use the remaining ganache to sandwich the cake together and spread smoothly and evenly over the top and sides of the cake.

5 Melt the cake covering and spread it over a large sheet of baking parchment. Let cool until just set. Cut into strips a little wider than the height of the cake. Place the strips around the edge of the cake, overlapping them slightly.

6 Using a pastry bag fitted with a fine tip pipe the reserved ganache in tear drops or shells to cover the top of the cake. Let the finished cake chill for 1 hour in the refrigerator before serving.

chocolate truffle cake

serves twelve

⅓ cup butter

⅓ cup superfine sugar

2 eggs, beaten lightly

⅔ cup self-rising flour

½ tsp baking powder

¼ cup unsweetened cocoa

½ cup ground almonds

TRUFFLE TOPPING

12 oz/350 g semisweet chocolate

½ cup butter

1¼ cups heavy cream

1¼ cups plain cake crumbs

3 tbsp dark rum

TO DECORATE

Cape gooseberries

1¾ oz/50 g semisweet chocolate,
    melted

1 Lightly grease an 8-inch/20-cm round springform cake pan and line the bottom. Beat the butter and sugar together until light and fluffy. Gradually add the eggs to the creamed butter and sugar, beating well after each addition.

2 Sift the flour, baking powder, and cocoa together and fold into the mixture along with the ground almonds. Pour into the prepared pan and bake in a preheated oven, 350°F/180°C, for 20–25 minutes or until springy to the touch. Let the cake cool slightly in the pan, then transfer to a wire rack to cool completely. Wash and dry the pan and return the cooled cake to the pan.

3 To make the topping, heat the chocolate, butter, and cream in a heavy-based pan over low heat and stir until smooth. Cool, then let chill for 30 minutes. Beat well with a wooden spoon and chill for another 30 minutes. Beat the mixture again, then add the cake crumbs and rum, beating until well combined. Spoon the topping over the sponge cake and let chill for 3 hours.

4 Meanwhile, dip the Cape gooseberries in the melted chocolate until partially covered. Set aside on baking parchment to set. Transfer the cake to a serving plate, decorate with the chocolate-dipped Cape gooseberries and serve.

bûche de noël

serves ten

CAKE

4 eggs

½ cup superfine sugar

⅔ cup self-rising flour

2 tbsp unsweetened cocoa

FROSTING

5½ oz/150 g semisweet chocolate

2 egg yolks

⅔ cup milk

½ cup butter

4 tbsp confectioners' sugar

2 tbsp rum, optional

TO DECORATE

a little white glacé or royal frosting

confectioners' sugar, for dusting

holly leaves

1 Grease and line a 12 x 9-inch/ 30 x 23-cm jelly roll pan.

2 Beat the eggs and superfine sugar in a bowl with an electric mixer for 10 minutes or until the mixture is very light and foamy and the whisk leaves a trail. Sift the flour and cocoa and fold in. Pour into the prepared pan and bake in a preheated oven, 400°F/200°C, for 12 minutes or until springy to the touch. Turn out onto baking parchment sprinkled with a little superfine sugar. Peel off the lining parchment and trim the edges. Cut a small slit halfway into the cake, ½ inch/ 1 cm from one of the short ends. Starting at that end, roll up tightly, enclosing the parchment. Place on a wire rack to cool.

3 To make the frosting, break the chocolate into pieces and melt in a heatproof bowl set over a pan of hot water. Beat in the egg yolks, whisk in the milk and cook stirring until the mixture thickens enough to coat the back of a wooden spoon. Cover with dampened waxed paper and cool. Beat the butter and sugar until pale. Beat in the custard and rum (if using).

4 Unroll the sponge, spread with one-third of the frosting, and roll up. Place on a serving plate. Spread the remaining frosting over the cake and mark with a fork to give the effect of bark. Let the frosting set. Pipe white frosting to form the rings of the log. Sprinkle with sugar and decorate.

chocolate bread dessert

serves four

6 thick slices white bread, crusts
removed

scant 2 cups milk

6 fl oz/175 ml canned evaporated
milk

2 tbsp unsweetened cocoa

2 eggs

2 tbsp brown sugar

1 tsp vanilla extract

confectioners' sugar, for dusting

HOT FUDGE SAUCE

2 oz/55 g semisweet chocolate,
broken into pieces

1 tbsp unsweetened cocoa

2 tbsp light corn syrup

¼ cup butter or margarine

2 tbsp brown sugar

⅔ cup milk

1 tbsp cornstarch

1 Grease a shallow ovenproof dish.
Cut the bread into squares and
layer them in the dish.

2 Put the milk, evaporated milk,
and unsweetened cocoa in a pan
and heat gently, stirring occasionally,
until the mixture is lukewarm.

3 Whisk the eggs, sugar, and
vanilla extract together. Add the
warm milk mixture and beat well.

4 Pour into the prepared dish,
making sure that all the bread
is completely covered. Cover the dish
with plastic wrap and let chill in the
refrigerator for 1–2 hours.

5 Bake the dessert in a preheated
oven 350°F/180°C, for 35–40
minutes, until set. Let stand for
5 minutes.

6 To make the sauce, put all the
ingredients into a pan, heat
gently, stirring constantly until smooth.

7 Dust the dessert with
confectioners' sugar and serve
immediately with the hot fudge sauce.

chocolate layer log

serves eight

½ cup soft margarine

½ cup superfine sugar

2 eggs

¾ cup self-rising flour

¼ cup unsweetened cocoa

2 tbsp milk

WHITE CHOCOLATE BUTTER CREAM

2¾ oz/75 g white chocolate

2 tbsp milk

⅔ cup butter

¾ cup confectioners' sugar

2 tbsp orange-flavored liqueur

quick chocolate curls (see page 7),
    to decorate

1 Grease and line the sides of two 14-oz/400-g food cans.

2 Beat the margarine and sugar together in a bowl until light and fluffy. Gradually add the eggs, beating well after each addition. Sift the flour and cocoa together and fold into the cake mixture. Fold in the milk.

3 Divide the mixture between the prepared cans. Stand the cans on a cookie sheet and bake in a preheated oven, 350°F/180°C, for

40 minutes or until springy to the touch. Let cool for about 5 minutes in the cans, then turn out and cool completely on a wire rack.

4 Meanwhile, make the butter cream. Put the chocolate and milk in a pan and heat gently until the chocolate has melted, stirring until well combined. Let cool slightly. Beat the butter and confectioners' sugar together until light and fluffy. Beat in the orange liqueur. Gradually beat in the chocolate mixture.

5 Cut both cakes into ½-inch/1-cm thick slices, then reassemble them by sandwiching the slices together with some of the butter cream.

6 Place the cake on a serving plate and spread the remaining butter cream over the top and sides. Decorate with chocolate curls then serve, cut diagonally into slices.

chocolate & apricot squares

serves twelve

½ cup butter

6 oz/175 g white chocolate,
    chopped

4 eggs

½ cup superfine sugar

1¾ cups all-purpose flour, sifted

1 tsp baking powder

pinch of salt

3½ oz/100 g no-soak dried apricots,
    chopped

1 Lightly grease a 9-inch/20-cm square cake pan and line the bottom with baking parchment.

2 Melt the butter and chocolate in a heatproof bowl set over a pan of simmering water. Stir frequently with a wooden spoon until the mixture is smooth and glossy. Let the chocolate mixture cool slightly.

3 Beat the eggs and superfine sugar into the butter and chocolate mixture until well combined.

4 Fold in the flour, baking powder, salt, and chopped dried apricots, and mix together well.

5 Pour the mixture into the pan and bake in a preheated oven, 350°F/180°C, for 25–30 minutes.

6 The center of the cake may not be completely firm when you take it out of the oven, but it will set as it cools. Let it cool in the pan.

7 When the cake is completely cold turn it out of the pan and carefully slice into squares or bars to serve.

Hot Desserts

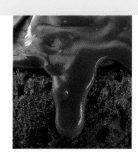

Chocolate is comforting at any time but no more so than when served in a steaming hot dessert. It is hard to think of anything more warming, comforting, and homely than tucking into a steamed hot Chocolate Fudge Dessert or a Hot Chocolate Soufflé, and children will love the chocolate Bread & Butter Dessert. In fact, there are several old favorite recipes that have been given the chocolate treatment, bringing them right up to date and putting them firmly on every chocolate lover's map.

When you are feeling in need of something a little more sophisticated, try the new-style Chocolate Apple Crêpe Stacks, or Chocolate Pear & Almond Tart, or Chocolate Zabaglione for an elegant creamy, warm dessert set to get your taste buds in a whirl!

mini chocolate gingers

serves four

generous ⅓ cup soft margarine

¾ cup self-rising flour, sifted

½ cup superfine sugar

2 eggs

¼ cup unsweetened cocoa, sifted

1 oz/25 g semisweet chocolate

1¾ oz/50 g preserved ginger

CHOCOLATE CUSTARD

2 egg yolks

1 tbsp superfine sugar

1 tbsp cornstarch

1¼ cups milk

3½ oz/100 g semisweet chocolate, broken into pieces

confectioners' sugar, for dusting

1 Lightly grease 4 small individual ovenproof bowls. Place the margarine, flour, sugar, eggs, and cocoa in a mixing bowl and beat until well combined and smooth. Chop the chocolate and preserved ginger and stir into the mixture, ensuring they are well combined.

2 Spoon the cake mixture into the prepared bowls and smooth the top. The mixture should three-quarters fill the bowls. Cover the bowls with discs of baking parchment and cover with a pleated sheet of foil. Steam the mini chocolate ginger for 45 minutes until the sponges are cooked and springy to the touch.

3 Meanwhile, make the custard. Beat the egg yolks, sugar, and cornstarch together to form a smooth paste. Heat the milk until boiling and pour over the egg mixture. Return to the pan and cook over very low heat, stirring until thick. Remove from the heat and beat in the chocolate. Stir until the chocolate melts.

4 Lift the mini chocolate gingers from the steamer, run a knife around the edge of the bowls, and carefully turn out onto serving plates. Dust each chocolate ginger with sugar and drizzle chocolate custard over the top. Serve the remaining chocolate custard separately.

chocolate queen of desserts

serves four

1¾ oz/50 g semisweet chocolate

2 cups chocolate-flavored milk

1⅔ cups fresh white bread crumbs

½ cup superfine sugar

2 eggs, separated

4 tbsp black cherry jelly

VARIATION

If you prefer, add ½ cup shredded coconut to the bread crumbs and omit the jelly.

1 Break the chocolate into small pieces and place in a pan with the chocolate-flavored milk. Heat gently, stirring until the chocolate melts. Bring almost to a boil, then remove the pan from the heat.

2 Place the bread crumbs in a large mixing bowl with 5 teaspoons of the sugar. Pour over the chocolate milk and mix well to incorporate. Beat in the egg yolks.

3 Spoon into a 5-cup pie dish and bake in a preheated oven, 350°F/180°C, for 25–30 minutes or until set and firm to the touch.

4 Whisk the egg whites in a large clean bowl until standing in soft peaks. Gradually whisk in the remaining superfine sugar and whisk until you have a glossy, thick meringue.

5 Spread the jelly over the chocolate mixture and pile the meringue on top. Return to the oven for about 15 minutes or until the meringue is crisp and golden.

chocolate eve's dessert

serves four

2 eating apples, peeled, cored, and
    sliced thickly

8 oz/225 g fresh or frozen
    raspberries

4 tbsp seedless raspberry jelly

2 tbsp port, optional

SPONGE TOPPING

4 tbsp soft margarine

4 tbsp superfine sugar

⅔ cup self-rising flour, sifted

1¾ oz/50 g white chocolate, grated

1 egg

2 tbsp milk

BITTER CHOCOLATE SAUCE

3 oz/85 g semisweet chocolate

⅔ cup light cream

VARIATION

Use semisweet chocolate in the
sponge and top with apricot
halves, covered with peach
schnapps and apricot jelly.

1 Place the apple slices and
    raspberries in a shallow 5-cup
ovenproof dish and set aside while you
warm the jelly and port (if using).

2 Place the raspberry jelly and
    port in a small pan and heat
gently until the jelly melts and
combines with the port. Pour the
mixture over the fruit.

3 Place all of the ingredients for the
    sponge topping in a large mixing
bowl and beat thoroughly with an
electric mixer until the mixture is
completely smooth.

4 Spoon the sponge mixture over
    the fruit and smooth the top. Bake
in a preheated oven, 350°F/180°C, for
40–45 minutes or until the sponge is
springy to the touch.

5 To make the sauce, break the
    chocolate into small pieces and
place in a heavy-based pan with the
cream. Heat gently, beating until a
smooth sauce is formed. Serve the
sauce warm with the dessert.

bread & butter dessert

serves four

8 oz/225 g brioche

1 tbsp butter

⅓ cup semisweet chocolate chips

1 egg, plus 2 egg yolks

4 tbsp superfine sugar

15 fl oz/425 ml canned light
evaporated milk

1 Cut the brioche into thin slices using a sharp knife. Lightly butter one side of each brioche slice.

2 Place a layer of brioche, buttered-side down, in the bottom of a shallow ovenproof dish. Sprinkle a few chocolate chips over the top.

3 Continue layering the brioche and chocolate chips, finishing with a layer of bread on top.

4 Whisk the egg, egg yolks, and sugar together until well combined. Heat the milk in a small pan until it just starts to simmer. Gradually add to the egg mixture, whisking well.

5 Pour the custard over the bread and let stand for 5 minutes. Press the brioche down into the milk.

6 Place the dessert in a roasting pan and fill with boiling water to come halfway up the side of the dish (this is known as a bain-marie). Bake in a preheated oven, 350°F/180°C, for 30 minutes or until the custard has set. Let the dessert cool for about 5 minutes before serving.

VARIATION

For a double chocolate dessert, heat the milk with 1 tablespoon of unsweetened cocoa, stirring until dissolved. Continue from step 4.

chocolate fruit crumble

serves four

14 oz/400 g canned apricots in
fruit juice

1 lb/450 g tart cooking apples,
peeled and sliced thickly

¾ cup all-purpose flour

6 tbsp butter

⅔ cup porridge oats

4 tbsp superfine sugar

⅔ cup semisweet chocolate chips

VARIATION

Other fruits can be used to make
this crumble—fresh pears mixed
with fresh or frozen raspberries
work well. If you do not use
canned fruit, add 4 tablespoons
of orange juice to the fresh fruit.

1 Lightly grease an ovenproof dish
with a little butter.

2 Drain the apricots, reserving
4 tablespoons of the juice. Place
the apples and apricots in the prepared
ovenproof dish with the reserved
apricot juice and toss to mix.

3 Sift the flour into a mixing bowl.
Cut the butter into small cubes
and rub in with your fingertips until the
mixture resembles fine bread crumbs.
Stir in the porridge oats, sugar, and
chocolate chips.

4 Sprinkle the crumble mixture over
the apples and apricots and
smooth the top roughly. Do not press
the crumble into the fruit.

5 Bake in a preheated oven,
350°F/180°C, for 40–45 minutes
or until the topping is golden. Serve
the crumble hot or cold.

chocolate & banana crêpes

serves four

3 large bananas

6 tbsp orange juice

grated rind of 1 orange

2 tbsp orange- or banana-flavored
    liqueur

HOT CHOCOLATE SAUCE

1 tbsp unsweetened cocoa

2 tsp cornstarch

3 tbsp milk

1½ oz/40 g semisweet chocolate

1 tbsp butter

½ cup light corn syrup

¼ tsp vanilla extract

CRÊPES

¾ cup all-purpose flour

1 tbsp unsweetened cocoa

1 egg

1 tsp corn oil

1¼ cups milk

oil, for cooking

1 Peel and slice the bananas and arrange them in a dish with the orange juice and rind and the liqueur. Set the bananas aside.

2 Mix the cocoa and cornstarch in a bowl, then stir in the milk. Break the semisweet chocolate into pieces and place in a pan with the butter and light corn syrup. Heat gently, stirring until well blended. Add the cocoa mixture and bring to a boil over gentle heat, stirring. Simmer for 1 minute, then remove from the heat and stir in the vanilla extract.

3 To make the crêpes, sift the flour and cocoa into a mixing bowl and make a well in the center. Add the egg and oil. Gradually whisk in the milk to form a smooth batter. Heat a little oil in a heavy-based skillet and pour off any excess. Pour in a little batter and tilt the pan to coat the bottom. Cook over medium heat until the underside is browned. Flip over and cook the other side. Slide the crêpe out of the skillet and keep warm. Repeat until all the crêpe batter has been used. Keep the crêpes warm.

4 To serve, re-heat the chocolate sauce for 1–2 minutes. Fill the crêpes with the bananas and fold in half or into triangles. Pour a little chocolate sauce over the crêpes and serve immediately.

poached pears in chocolate

6 firm ripe pears

½ cup superfine sugar

2 cinnamon sticks

rind of 1 orange

2 cloves

1 bottle rosé wine

CHOCOLATE SAUCE

6 oz/175 g semisweet chocolate

9 oz/250 g mascarpone cheese

2 tbsp orange-flavored liqueur

COOK'S TIP

There is no need to waste the poaching liquid. Boil it rapidly in a clean pan for about 10 minutes to reduce to a syrup. Use the syrup to sweeten a fresh fruit salad or spoon it over ice cream.

1 Carefully peel the pears, leaving the stalks intact.

2 Place the sugar, cinnamon sticks, orange rind, cloves, and wine in a pan that will hold the 6 pears snugly.

3 Heat gently until the sugar has dissolved, then add the pears to the liquid and bring to a simmer. Cover and poach gently for 20 minutes. If serving cold, let the pears cool in the liquid, then chill until required. If serving hot, leave the pears in the hot liquid while preparing the chocolate sauce.

4 To make the sauce, melt the chocolate. Beat the mascapone cheese and the liqueur together. Beat the cheese mixture into the melted chocolate.

5 Remove the pears from the poaching liquid and place on a serving plate. Add a spoonful of sauce on the side and serve the rest separately. Alternatively, pipe a rosette of the sauce onto each plate.

chocolate pear & almond tart

serves six

¾ cup all-purpose flour

¼ cup ground almonds

5 tbsp block margarine

about 3 tbsp water

FILLING

14 oz/400 g canned pear halves in
    fruit juice

4 tbsp butter

4 tbsp superfine sugar

2 eggs, beaten

1 cup ground almonds

2 tbsp unsweetened cocoa

a few drops of almond extract

confectioners' sugar, for dusting

CHOCOLATE SAUCE

4 tbsp superfine sugar

3 tbsp light corn syrup

generous ⅓ cup water

6 oz/175 g semisweet chocolate,
    broken into pieces

2 tbsp butter

1 Lightly grease an 8-inch/20-cm tart pan. Sift the flour into a mixing bowl and stir in the almonds. Rub in the margarine with your fingertips until the mixture resembles bread crumbs. Add enough water to mix to a soft dough. Cover, chill in the freezer for 10 minutes, then roll out and use to line the pan. Prick the bottom and chill.

2 Meanwhile, make the filling. Drain the pears well. Beat the butter and sugar until light and fluffy. Beat in the eggs. Fold in the almonds, cocoa, and almond extract. Spread the chocolate mixture in the pie shell and arrange the pears on top, pressing down lightly. Bake in the center of a preheated oven, 400°F/200°C, for 30 minutes or until the filling has risen. Cool slightly and transfer to a serving dish, if wished. Dust with sugar.

3 To make the chocolate sauce, place the sugar, syrup, and water in a small pan and heat gently, stirring until the sugar dissolves. Boil gently for 1 minute. Remove from the heat, add the chocolate and butter, and stir until melted. Serve the sauce immediately with the tart.

chocolate apple pie

serves six

CHOCOLATE PIE DOUGH

4 tbsp unsweetened cocoa

1¾ cups all-purpose flour

generous ⅓ cup softened butter

4 tbsp superfine sugar

2 egg yolks

a few drops of vanilla extract

cold water, for mixing

FILLING

1 lb 10 oz/750 g tart cooking apples

2 tbsp butter

½ tsp ground cinnamon

⅓ cup semisweet chocolate chips

a little egg white, beaten

½ tsp superfine sugar

whipped cream or vanilla ice cream,
    to serve (optional)

1 To make the pie dough, sift
the cocoa and flour into a mixing
bowl and rub in the butter until the
mixture resembles fine bread crumbs.
Stir in the sugar. Add the egg yolks,
vanilla extract, and enough water to
mix to a dough.

2 Roll out the dough on a lightly
floured counter and use to line a
deep 8-inch/20-cm flan or cake pan.

Let chill for 30 minutes. Roll out any
trimmings and cut out some pie dough
leaves to decorate the top of the pie.

3 Peel, core, and thickly slice the
apples. Place half of the apple
slices in a pan with the butter and
cinnamon and cook over gentle heat,
stirring occasionally, until the apples
have softened.

4 Stir in the uncooked apple slices,
let cool slightly, then stir in the
chocolate chips. Prick the bottom of the
pie shell and pile the apple mixture into
it. Arrange the pie dough leaves on top.
Brush the leaves with a little egg white
and sprinkle with superfine sugar.

5 Bake the pie in a preheated oven,
350°F/180°C, for 35 minutes or
until the pie crust is crisp. Serve the
chocolate apple pie warm or cold, in
thick slices, with a spoonful of whipped
cream or vanilla ice cream on the side
if desired.

chocolate fudge dessert

serves six

generous ⅓ cup soft margarine

1¼ cups self-rising flour

½ cup light corn syrup

3 eggs

¼ cup unsweetened cocoa

CHOCOLATE FUDGE SAUCE

3½ oz/100 g semisweet chocolate

½ cup condensed milk

4 tbsp heavy cream

1 Lightly grease a 5-cup heatproof bowl.

2 Place the ingredients for the sponge in a separate mixing bowl and beat until well combined and smooth.

3 Spoon into the prepared bowl and smooth the top. Cover with a disk of waxed paper and tie a pleated sheet of foil over the bowl. Steam for 1½–2 hours, until the sponge is cooked and springy to the touch.

4 To make the sauce, break the chocolate into small pieces and place in a small pan with the condensed milk. Heat gently, stirring until the chocolate melts.

5 Remove the pan from the heat and stir in the cream.

6 To serve the dessert, turn it out onto a serving plate and pour over a little of the chocolate fudge sauce. Serve the remaining sauce separately.

chocolate meringue pie

serves six

8 oz/225 g semisweet chocolate
   graham crackers

4 tbsp butter

FILLING

3 egg yolks

4 tbsp superfine sugar

4 tbsp cornstarch

2½ cups milk

3½ oz/100 g semisweet chocolate,
   melted

MERINGUE

2 egg whites

½ cup superfine sugar

¼ tsp vanilla extract

1 Place the graham crackers in a plastic bag and crush with a rolling pin. Pour into a mixing bowl. Melt the butter and stir it into the cracker crumbs until well mixed. Press the mixture firmly into the bottom and up the sides of a 23-cm/9-inch tart pan or dish.

2 To make the filling, beat the egg yolks, superfine sugar, and cornstarch in a large bowl until they form a smooth paste, adding a little of the milk if necessary. Heat the milk until almost boiling, then slowly pour it onto the egg mixture, whisking well.

3 Return the mixture to the pan and cook gently, whisking constantly, until it thickens. Remove from the heat. Whisk in the melted chocolate, then pour it onto the graham cracker pie shell. Smooth out the filling.

4 To make the meringue, whisk the egg whites in a large mixing bowl until standing in soft peaks. Gradually whisk in about two-thirds of the sugar until the mixture is stiff and glossy. Fold the remaining sugar and vanilla extract into the meringue.

5 Spread the meringue over the filling, swirling the surface with the back of a spoon to give it an attractive finish. Bake in the center of a preheated oven, 325°F/160°C, for 30 minutes or until the meringue is golden. Serve the pie hot or just warm.

apple crêpe stacks

serves four

2 cups all-purpose flour

1½ tsp baking powder

4 tbsp superfine sugar

1 egg

1 tbsp butter, melted

1¼ cups milk

1 eating apple

⅓ cup semisweet chocolate chips

Chocolate Sauce (see page 82) or

    maple syrup, to serve

COOK'S TIP

To keep the cooked crêpes warm, pile them on top of each other with waxed paper in between to prevent them from sticking to one another.

1 Sift the flour and baking powder into a mixing bowl. Stir in the superfine sugar. Make a well in the center and add the egg and melted butter. Gradually whisk in the milk to form a smooth batter.

2 Peel, core, and grate the apple and stir it into the batter together with the chocolate chips.

3 Heat a griddle pan or heavy-based skillet over medium heat and grease it lightly. For each crêpe, place about 2 tablespoons of the batter onto the griddle or skillet and spread to make a 3-inch/7.5-cm circle.

4 Cook for a few minutes until you see bubbles appear on the surface of the crêpe. Turn over and cook for another minute. Remove from the pan and keep warm. Repeat with the remaining batter to make about 12 crêpes.

5 To serve, stack 3 or 4 crêpes on an individual serving plate and serve them with the Chocolate Sauce, or maple syrup.

chocolate fondue

serves four

CHOCOLATE FONDUE

8 oz/225 g semisweet chocolate

generous ¾ cup heavy cream

2 tbsp brandy

TO SERVE

selection of fruit

white and pink marshmallows

sweet cookies

1 Break the chocolate into small pieces and place in a small pan with the cream.

2 Heat the mixture gently, stirring constantly, until the chocolate has melted and blended with the cream.

3 Remove the pan from the heat and stir in the brandy.

4 Pour into a fondue pot or a small flameproof dish and keep warm, preferably over a small burner.

5 Serve with a selection of fruit, marshmallows, and cookies for dipping. The fruit and marshmallows can be spiked on fondue forks, wooden skewers, or ordinary forks.

COOK'S TIP

To prepare the fruit for dipping, cut larger fruit into bite-size pieces. Fruit that discolors, such as bananas, apples, and pears, should be dipped in a little lemon juice as soon as it is cut.

chocolate ravioli

serves four

1½ cups all-purpose flour

4 tbsp unsweetened cocoa

2 tbsp confectioners' sugar

2 eggs, beaten lightly, plus 1 extra
    beaten egg for brushing

1 tbsp vegetable oil

FILLING

6 oz/175 g white chocolate, broken
    into pieces

1 cup mascarpone cheese

1 egg

1 tbsp finely chopped preserved
    ginger

fresh mint sprigs, to decorate

heavy cream, to serve

1 Sift the flour, cocoa, and sugar together onto a clean counter. Make a well in the center and pour the 2 beaten eggs and the oil into it. Gradually draw in the flour with your fingertips until it is fully incorporated. Alternatively, sift the flour, cocoa, and sugar into a food processor, add the eggs and oil and process until mixed. Knead the dough until it is smooth and elastic, then cover with plastic wrap and place in the refrigerator for 30 minutes to chill.

2 Meanwhile, to make the filling, put the white chocolate in the top of a double boiler or in a heatproof bowl set over a pan of barely simmering water. When the chocolate has melted, remove it from the heat and let cool slightly, then beat in the mascarpone cheese and the egg. Stir in the preserved ginger.

3 Remove the pasta dough from the refrigerator, cut it in half, and keep one half tightly wrapped in plastic wrap. Roll out the first half of the dough into a rectangle on a lightly floured counter, then cover with a clean, damp dish towel. Roll out the other half into a rectangle. Spoon the chocolate and ginger filling into a pastry bag and pipe small mounds in even rows at intervals of about 1½ inches/4 cm over 1 dough rectangle. Brush the spaces between the mounds with beaten egg, then, using a rolling pin to lift it, position

the second dough rectangle on top of the first. Press firmly between the mounds with your finger to seal and push out any pockets of air. Cut the dough into squares around the mounds using a serrated ravioli or dough cutter or a sharp knife. Transfer the ravioli to a lightly floured dish towel and let rest for 30 minutes.

4 Bring a large pan of water to a boil, then lower the heat to medium and cook the ravioli, in batches, stirring to prevent them from sticking together, for 4–5 minutes, until tender, but still firm to the bite. Remove with a slotted spoon. Serve immediately on individual plates, garnished with mint sprigs, and hand the cream separately.

saucy chocolate dessert

serves four

1¼ cups milk

2¾ oz/75 g semisweet chocolate

½ tsp vanilla extract

½ cup superfine sugar

generous ⅓ cup butter

1¼ cups self-rising flour

2 tbsp unsweetened cocoa

confectioners' sugar, for dusting

CHOCOLATE SAUCE

3 tbsp unsweetened cocoa

⅓ cup brown sugar

1¼ cups boiling water

1 Lightly grease a 3¼-cup ovenproof dish with butter.

2 Place the milk in a small pan. Break the chocolate into small pieces and add to the milk. Heat gently, stirring until the chocolate melts. Let the mixture cool slightly. Stir in the vanilla extract.

3 Beat the superfine sugar and butter together in a bowl until light and fluffy. Sift the flour and cocoa together. Add to the bowl with the chocolate milk and beat until smooth. Pour into the prepared dish.

4 To make the chocolate sauce, mix the cocoa and sugar together in a small bowl. Add a little boiling water to the mixture and stir to a smooth paste, then stir in the remaining boiling water. Carefully pour the chocolate sauce over the surface of the dessert mixture but do not mix in.

5 Place the dish on a cookie sheet and bake in a preheated oven, 350°F/180°C, for 40 minutes or until the dessert is dry on top and springy to the touch. Let the dessert stand for about 5 minutes, then dust lightly with a little confectioners' sugar just before serving.

pecan fudge ring

serves six

FUDGE SAUCE

3 tbsp butter

3 tbsp brown sugar

4 tbsp light corn syrup

2 tbsp milk

1 tbsp unsweetened cocoa

1½ oz/40 g semisweet chocolate

⅓ cup finely chopped pecan nuts

CAKE

generous ⅓ cup soft margarine

⅔ cup brown sugar

1 cup self-rising flour

2 eggs

2 tbsp milk

1 tbsp light corn syrup

1 Lightly grease an 8-inch/20-cm ovenproof ring pan.

2 To make the fudge sauce, place the butter, sugar, syrup, milk, and cocoa in a small pan and heat gently, stirring until combined.

3 Break the chocolate into pieces, add to the mixture and stir until melted. Stir in the chopped nuts. Pour into the bottom of the pan and let cool.

4 To make the cake, place all of the ingredients in a large mixing bowl and beat thoroughly until smooth. Carefully spoon the cake mixture over the chocolate fudge sauce in the bottom of the pan.

5 Bake in a preheated oven, 350°F/180°C, for 35 minutes or until the cake is springy to the touch.

6 Let the fudge ring cool in the pan for 5 minutes, then turn out onto a serving plate and serve.

hot chocolate soufflé

serves four

3½ oz/100 g semisweet chocolate

1¼ cups milk

2 tbsp butter

4 large eggs, separated

1 tbsp cornstarch

4 tbsp superfine sugar

½ tsp vanilla extract

⅔ cup semisweet chocolate chips

superfine and confectioners' sugar,
   for dusting

CHOCOLATE CUSTARD

2 tbsp cornstarch

1 tbsp superfine sugar

2 cups milk

1¾ oz/50 g semisweet chocolate

1 Grease a 5-cup soufflé dish and sprinkle with superfine sugar. Break the chocolate into pieces.

2 Heat the milk with the butter in a pan until almost boiling. Mix the egg yolks, cornstarch, and superfine sugar in a bowl and pour on some of the hot milk, whisking. Return it to the pan and cook gently, stirring constantly, until thickened. Add the chocolate and stir until melted. Remove from the heat and stir in the extract.

3 Whisk the egg whites until standing in soft peaks. Fold half of the egg whites into the chocolate mixture. Fold in the rest with the chocolate chips. Pour into the dish

and bake in a preheated oven, 350°F/180°C, for 40–45 minutes, until well risen.

4 Meanwhile, make the custard. Put the cornstarch and sugar in a small bowl and mix to a smooth paste with a little of the milk. Heat the remaining milk until almost boiling. Pour a little of the hot milk onto the cornstarch, mix well, then pour back into the pan. Cook gently, stirring until thickened. Break the chocolate into pieces and add to the custard, stirring gently until melted.

5 Dust the soufflé with sugar and serve immediately with the chocolate custard.

fudge dessert

serves four

4 tbsp margarine

½ cup brown sugar

2 eggs, beaten

1¼ cups milk

⅓ cup chopped walnuts

¼ cup all-purpose flour

2 tbsp unsweetened cocoa

confectioners' sugar and

    unsweetened cocoa, for dusting

1 Lightly grease a 4-cup ovenproof dish. Set aside.

2 Cream the margarine and sugar together in a large mixing bowl until fluffy. Beat in the eggs.

3 Gradually stir in the milk and add the walnuts.

4 Sift the flour and cocoa into the mixture and fold in gently with a metal spoon, until well mixed.

5 Spoon the mixture into the dish and cook in a preheated oven, 350°F/180°C, for 35–40 minutes or until the sponge is cooked.

6 Dust with confectioners' sugar and cocoa and serve.

chocolate zabaglione

serves four

4 egg yolks

4 tbsp superfine sugar

1¾ oz/50 g semisweet chocolate

½ cup Marsala wine

unsweetened cocoa, for dusting

COOK'S TIP

Make the dessert just before serving as it will separate if you let it stand. If it starts to curdle, remove it from the heat immediately and place it in a bowl of cold water to stop the cooking. Whisk the chocolate zabaglione furiously until the mixture comes together.

1 Whisk the egg yolks and superfine sugar together in a mixing bowl until you have a very pale mixture, using an electric mixer.

2 Grate the chocolate finely and fold into the egg yolk and superfine sugar mixture.

3 Fold the Marsala wine into the chocolate mixture.

4 Place the mixing bowl over a pan of gently simmering water and set the electric whisk on the lowest speed or change to a hand-held balloon whisk. Cook gently, whisking constantly until the mixture thickens. Take care not to overcook or the mixture will curdle. If this happens, follow the Cook's Tip.

5 Spoon the hot mixture into warmed individual glass dishes or coffee cups (as here) and dust with cocoa. Serve the zabaglione as soon as possible after you make it so that it is still warm, light, and fluffy.

steamed coffee sponge

serves four

2 tbsp margarine

2 tbsp brown sugar

2 eggs

⅓ cup all-purpose flour

¾ tsp baking powder

6 tbsp milk

1 tsp coffee extract

SAUCE

1¼ cups milk

1 tbsp brown sugar

1 tsp unsweetened cocoa

2 tbsp cornstarch

1 Lightly grease a 2½-cup heatproof bowl. Cream the margarine and sugar until fluffy and beat in the eggs.

2 Gradually stir the flour and baking powder and then the milk and coffee extract into the margarine and sugar, to make a smooth batter.

3 Spoon the mixture into the prepared heatproof bowl and cover with a pleated piece of baking parchment and then a pleated piece of foil, securing around the bowl with string. Place in a steamer or large pan and half fill with boiling water. Cover and steam for 1–1¼ hours or until cooked through.

4 To make the sauce, put the milk, soft brown sugar, and cocoa in a pan and heat until the sugar dissolves. Blend the cornstarch with 4 tablespoons of cold water to make a paste and stir into the pan. Bring to a boil, stirring until thickened. Cook over gentle heat for 1 minute.

5 Turn the coffee sponge carefully out onto a serving plate and spoon the chocolate sauce over the top. Serve.

COOK'S TIP

The sponge is covered with pleated paper and foil to allow it to rise. The foil will react with the steam and must therefore not be placed directly against the sponge.

chocolate dessert with rum

serves four

4 tbsp unsalted butter

1¼ cups self-rising flour

2 oz/55 g semisweet chocolate

¼ tsp vanilla extract

scant ⅔ cup superfine sugar

2 eggs, beaten lightly

5 tbsp milk

SAUCE

1¼ cups milk

2 tbsp cornstarch

2 tbsp superfine sugar

2 tbsp dark rum

1 Grease and flour a 5-cup ovenproof bowl. Put the butter, chocolate, and vanilla in the top of a double boiler or a heatproof bowl set over a pan of barely simmering water. Heat gently until melted, then remove from the heat and cool slightly. Stir the sugar into the chocolate mixture, then beat in the eggs. Sift in the flour, stir in the milk, and mix well. Pour the mixture into the prepared ovenproof bowl, cover the top with a pleated piece of foil, and tie with string. Steam for 1 hour, topping off with boiling water if necessary.

2 To make the sauce, pour the milk into a small pan set over medium heat. Stir in the cornstarch, then stir in the sugar until dissolved. Bring to a boil, stirring constantly, then lower the heat and let simmer until thickened and smooth. Remove from the heat and stir in the rum.

3 To serve, remove the sponge from the heat and discard the foil. Run a round-bladed knife around the side of the bowl, place a serving plate on top of the sponge, and, holding them together, carefully invert. Serve the dessert immediately, handing the rum sauce separately.

89

sticky chocolate sponges

serves six

½ cup butter, softened

1 cup brown sugar

3 eggs, beaten

pinch of salt

¼ cup unsweetened cocoa

1 cup self-rising flour

1 oz/25 g semisweet chocolate,
    chopped finely

2¾ oz/75 g white chocolate,
    chopped finely

SAUCE

⅔ cup heavy cream

½ cup brown sugar

2 tbsp butter

1 Lightly grease 6 individual ¾-cup individual dessert molds.

2 Cream the butter and sugar together in a bowl until pale and fluffy. Beat in the eggs a little at a time, beating well after each addition.

3 Sift the salt, cocoa, and flour into the creamed mixture, and fold through the mixture. Stir the chopped chocolate into the mixture until evenly combined throughout.

4 Divide the mixture between the prepared molds. Lightly grease 6 squares of foil and use them to cover the tops of the molds. Press around the edges to seal them.

5 Place the molds in a roasting pan and pour in boiling water to come halfway up the sides of the molds.

6 Bake in a preheated oven, 350°F/180°C, for 50 minutes or until a skewer inserted into the center of the sponges comes out clean.

7 Remove the molds from the roasting pan and set aside while you prepare the sauce.

8 To make the sauce, put the cream, sugar, and butter into a pan and bring to a boil over gentle heat. Simmer gently until the sugar has completely dissolved.

9 To serve, run a knife around the edge of each sponge, then turn out onto serving plates. Pour the sauce over the top of the chocolate sponges and serve immediately.

tropical fruit kabobs

serves four

DIP

4½ oz/125 g semisweet chocolate,
   broken into pieces

2 tbsp light corn syrup

1 tbsp unsweetened cocoa

1 tbsp cornstarch

generous ¾ cup milk

KABOBS

1 mango

1 papaya

2 kiwifruit

½ small pineapple

1 large banana

2 tbsp lemon juice

⅔ cup white rum

1 Put all the ingredients for the chocolate dip into a heavy-based pan. Heat over the barbecue grill or over low heat, stirring constantly, until thickened and smooth. Keep warm at the edge of the barbecue grill.

2 Slice the mango on each side of its large, flat pit. Cut the flesh into chunks, removing the peel. Halve, seed, and peel the papaya and cut it into chunks. Peel the kiwifruit and slice into chunks. Peel and cut the pineapple into chunks. Peel and slice the banana and dip the pieces in the lemon juice, turning them to coat evenly, to prevent it from discoloring.

3 Thread the pieces of fruit alternately onto 4 skewers. Place them in a shallow dish and pour over the rum. Set aside to soak up the flavor of the rum for at least 30 minutes, until ready to cook.

4 Cook the kabobs over the hot coals, turning frequently, for about 2 minutes, until seared. Serve, accompanied by the hot chocolate dip.

stuffed nectarines

serves six

3 oz/85 g bittersweet chocolate, chopped finely

1 cup amaretti cookie crumbs

1 tsp finely grated lemon rind

1 large egg, separated

6 tbsp Amaretto liqueur

6 nectarines, halved and pitted

1¼ cups white wine

2 oz/55 g light chocolate, grated

whipped cream or ice cream, to serve

1 Mix the chocolate, amaretti crumbs and lemon rind together in a large bowl. Lightly beat the egg white and add it to the mixture with half the Amaretto liqueur. Using a small sharp knife, slightly enlarge the cavities in the nectarines. Add the removed nectarine flesh to the chocolate and crumb mixture and mix together well.

2 Preheat the oven to 375°F/190°C. Place the nectarines, cut-side up, in an ovenproof dish just large enough to hold them in a single layer. Pile the chocolate and crumb mixture into the cavities, dividing it equally among them. Mix the wine and remaining Amaretto and pour it into the dish around the nectarines. Bake in a

preheated oven for 40–45 minutes, until the nectarines are tender. Transfer 2 nectarine halves to each individual serving plate and spoon over a little of the cooking juices. Sprinkle over the grated light chocolate and serve the nectarines immediately with whipped cream or, if you prefer, vanilla or chocolate ice cream.

banana empanadas

serves four

about 8 sheets of phyllo pastry, cut
into half lengthwise

melted butter, for brushing

2 ripe sweet bananas

1–2 tsp sugar

juice of ½ lemon

6–7 oz/175–200 g semisweet
chocolate, broken into pieces

confectioners' sugar and ground
cinnamon, for dusting

COOK'S TIP

You could use ready-made puff
pie dough instead of phyllo for
a more puffed-up effect.

1 Working one at a time, lay a long
rectangular sheet of phyllo pastry
out in front of you and then brush it all
over with butter.

2 Peel and dice the bananas and
place in a bowl. Add the sugar
and lemon juice and stir well to
combine. Stir in the chocolate.

3 Place 2 teaspoons of the banana
and chocolate mixture in one
corner of the phyllo pastry, then fold
over into a triangle shape to enclose
the filling. Continue to fold in a
triangular shape, until the pastry is
completely wrapped around the filling.

4 Dust the parcels with
confectioners' sugar and
cinnamon. Place them on a cookie
sheet and continue the process with
the remaining phyllo pastry and
banana or chocolate filling.

5 Bake in a preheated oven,
375°F/190°C, for 15 minutes or
until the empanadas are golden.
Remove from the oven and serve
immediately—warn people that the
filling is very hot.

chocolate fudge pears

serves four

4 pears

1–2 tbsp lemon juice

1¼ cups water

5 tbsp superfine sugar

2-inch/5-cm piece of cinnamon stick

2 cloves

scant 1 cup heavy cream

½ cup milk

scant 1 cup brown sugar

2 tbsp unsalted butter, diced

2 tbsp maple syrup

7 oz/200 g semisweet chocolate,
     broken into pieces

1 Peel the pears using a swivel vegetable peeler. Carefully cut out the cores from underneath, but leave the stalks intact because they look more attractive. Brush the pears with the lemon juice to prevent discoloration.

2 Pour the water into a large, heavy-based pan and add the superfine sugar. Stir over low heat until the sugar has dissolved. Add the pears, cinnamon, and cloves and bring to a boil. (Add a little more water if the pears are not almost covered.) Lower the heat and simmer for 20 minutes.

3 Meanwhile, pour the cream and milk into another heavy-based pan and add the brown sugar, butter, and maple syrup. Stir over low heat until the sugar has dissolved and the butter has melted. Bring to a boil, then boil, stirring, for 5 minutes, until thick and smooth. Remove from the heat and stir in the chocolate, a little at a time, waiting until each batch has melted before adding the next. Set aside.

4 Transfer the pears to serving plates. Bring the poaching syrup back to a boil and cook until reduced. Discard the cinnamon and cloves, then fold the syrup into the chocolate sauce. Pour over the pears and serve.

chocolate crêpes

serves six

⅔ cup all-purpose flour

1 tbsp unsweetened cocoa

1 tsp superfine sugar

2 eggs, beaten lightly

¾ cup milk

2 tsp dark rum

6 tbsp sweet butter

confectioners' sugar, for dusting

FILLING

5 tbsp heavy cream

8 oz/225 g semisweet chocolate

3 eggs, separated

2 tbsp superfine sugar

BERRY SAUCE

2 tbsp butter

4 tbsp superfine sugar

⅔ cup orange juice

2 cups mixed berries, such as
    raspberries, blackberries, and
    strawberries

3 tbsp white rum

1 To make the batter for the chocolate crêpes, sift the flour, cocoa, and superfine sugar into a bowl. Make a well in the center and add the eggs, beating them in a little at a time. Add the milk and beat until smooth. Stir in the rum.

2 Melt all the butter and stir 2 tablespoonfuls into the batter. Cover with plastic wrap and let stand for 30 minutes.

3 To cook the crêpes, brush the bottom of a 7-inch/18-cm crêpe pan or non-stick skillet with melted butter and set over medium heat. Stir the batter and pour 3 tablespoonfuls into the pan, swirling it to cover. Cook for 2 minutes or until the underside is golden, flip over, cook for 30 seconds, then slide on to a plate. Cook another 11 crêpes and stack interleaved with baking parchment.

4 For the filling, pour the cream into a heavy-based pan, add the chocolate and melt over low heat, stirring. Remove from the heat. Beat the egg yolks with half of the superfine sugar in a bowl until creamy, then beat in the chocolate cream.

5 Whisk the egg whites in a separate bowl until soft peaks form, add the rest of the superfine sugar and beat into stiff peaks. Stir a spoonful of the whites into the chocolate mixture, then fold the mixture into the remaining egg whites.

6 Brush a cookie sheet with melted butter. Spread 1 crêpe with 1 tablespoon of the filling, then fold it in half and in half again to make a triangle. Place on the cookie sheet. Repeat with the remaining crêpes. Brush the tops with the remaining melted butter and bake in a preheated oven 400°F/200°C for 20 minutes.

7 For the berry sauce, melt the butter in a heavy-based skillet over low heat, stir in the sugar, and cook until golden. Stir in the orange juice and cook until syrupy. Add the mixed berries to the pan and warm through, stirring gently. Add the rum, heat gently for 1 minute, then ignite. Shake the pan until the flames have died down. Transfer the flambéed crêpes to serving plates, and dust with confectioner's sugar. Add a little of the sauce and serve immediately.

chocolate cranberry sponge

serves four

4 tbsp unsalted butter

4 tbsp brown sugar, plus 2 tsp extra
    for sprinkling

¾ cup cranberries, thawed if frozen

1 large tart cooking apple

2 eggs, beaten lightly

⅔ cup self-rising flour

3 tbsp unsweetened cocoa

SAUCE

6 oz/175 g semisweet chocolate,
    broken into pieces

1¾ cups canned evaporated milk

1 tsp vanilla extract

½ tsp almond extract

1 Grease a 5-cup ovenproof bowl, sprinkle with brown sugar to coat the sides, and tip out any excess. Put the cranberries in a bowl. Peel, core, and dice the apple and mix with the cranberries. Put the fruit into the prepared ovenproof bowl.

2 Place the butter, brown sugar, and eggs in a large bowl. Sift in the flour and cocoa and beat well until thoroughly mixed. Pour the mixture into the ovenproof bowl on top of the fruit, cover the top with a pleated piece of foil, and tie with string. Steam for about 1 hour, until risen, topping off with boiling water if necessary.

3 Meanwhile, to make the sauce, put the semisweet chocolate and milk into the top of a double boiler or a heatproof bowl set over a pan of barely simmering water. Stir until the chocolate has melted, then remove from the heat. Whisk in the vanilla and almond extracts and continue to beat until the sauce is thick and smooth.

4 To serve, remove the sponge from the heat and discard the foil. Run a round-bladed knife around the side of the bowl, place a serving plate on top of the sponge and, holding them together, carefully invert. Serve the sponge immediately, handing the sauce separately.

chocolate castle puddings

serves four

3 tbsp butter

3 tbsp superfine sugar

1 large egg, beaten lightly

⅔ cup self-rising flour

2 oz/55 g semisweet chocolate,
  melted

SAUCE

2 tbsp unsweetened cocoa

2 tbsp cornstarch

⅔ cup light cream

1¼ cups milk

1–2 tbsp brown sugar

1 Grease 4 muffin cups or small heatproof bowls. In a mixing bowl, cream the butter and sugar together until pale and fluffy. Gradually add the egg, beating well after each addition.

2 Sift the flour into a separate bowl, fold it into the butter mixture with a metal spoon, then stir in the melted chocolate. Divide the mixture among the muffin cups, filling them to about two-thirds full to allow for expansion during cooking. Cover each cup with a circle of foil, and tie in place with string.

3 Bring a large pan of water to a boil and set a steamer over it. Place the muffin cups in the steamer and cook for 40 minutes. Check the water level from time to time and top off with boiling water necessary. Do not allow the pan to boil dry.

4 To make the sauce, put the cocoa, cornstarch, cream, and milk in a heavy-based pan. Bring to a boil, then lower the heat and simmer over low heat, whisking constantly, until thick and smooth. Cook for another 2–3 minutes, then stir in brown sugar to taste. Pour the sauce into a pitcher.

5 Lift the muffin cups out of the steamer and remove the foil circles from them. Run a knife blade around the sides of the cups and turn out the chocolate castles onto warmed individual plates. Serve immediately, handing the sauce separately.

italian drowned ice cream

serves four

2 cups freshly made espresso coffee

chocolate-coated coffee beans, to

decorate

VANILLA ICE CREAM

1 vanilla bean

6 large egg yolks

⅔ cup superfine sugar, or vanilla-

flavored sugar (sugar that has

been stored with a vanilla bean)

2¼ cups milk

1 cup plus 2 tbsp heavy cream

1 To make the vanilla ice cream, slit the vanilla bean lengthwise and using a knife scrape out the tiny brown seeds. Set aside.

2 Put the yolks and sugar into a heatproof bowl that will sit over a pan with plenty of room underneath. Beat the eggs and sugar together until thick and creamy.

3 Put the milk, cream, and vanilla pods in the pan over low heat and bring to a simmer. Pour the milk over the egg mixture, whisking. Pour 1 inch/2.5 cm of water in the bottom of a pan. Place the bowl on top, ensuring that the base does not touch the water. Turn the heat to medium–high.

4 Cook the mixture, stirring constantly, until it is thick enough to coat the back of the spoon. Remove the pan from the heat, transfer the mixture to a bowl, and let cool.

5 Churn the mixture in an ice-cream maker, following the manufacturer's instructions. Alternatively, place it in a freezerproof container and freeze for 1 hour. Turn out into a bowl and whisk to break up the ice crystals, then return to the freezer. Repeat the process 4 times at 30-minute intervals.

6 Transfer the ice cream to a freezerproof bowl, smooth the top, and cover with plastic wrap or foil. Freeze for up to 3 months.

7 Let soften in the refrigerator for 20 minutes before serving. Place scoops of ice cream in each bowl. Pour over coffee and sprinkle with coffee beans.

chocolate fruit dip

serves four

selection of fruit (choose from
    oranges, bananas, strawberries,
    pineapple chunks (fresh or
    canned), apricots (fresh or
    canned), apples, pears, kiwifruit)
1 tbsp lemon juice
CHOCOLATE SAUCE
4 tbsp butter
1¾ oz/50 g semisweet chocolate,
    broken into small cubes
½ tbsp unsweetened cocoa
2 tbsp light corn syrup
BASTE
4 tbsp honey
grated rind and juice of ½ orange

1 To make the chocolate sauce,
place the butter, chocolate, cocoa,
and syrup in a small pan. Heat gently
on a stove or at the side of a barbecue
grill, stirring constantly, until all of the
ingredients have melted and are well
combined.

2 To prepare the fruit, peel and
core if necessary, then cut into
large, bite-size pieces or wedges as
appropriate. Dip apples, pears, and
bananas in lemon juice to prevent
discoloration. Thread the pieces of
fruit onto skewers.

3 To make the baste, mix the honey,
orange rind, and orange juice
together, heat gently if required, and
brush over the fruit.

4 Grill the fruit skewers over warm
coals for 5–10 minutes until hot.
Serve the skewers with the chocolate
dipping sauce.

chocolate fudge sauce

makes scant 1 cup

⅔ cup heavy cream

4 tbsp unsalted butter, diced

3 tbsp superfine sugar

6 oz/175 g white chocolate, broken
    into pieces

2 tbsp brandy

1 Pour the cream into the top of a double boiler or a heatproof glass bowl set over a pan of barely simmering water. Add the butter and superfine sugar to the cream and stir constantly with a wooden spoon until the mixture is smooth. Remove the pan from the heat.

2 Stir in the chocolate, a few pieces at a time, waiting until each batch has melted before adding the next. Add the brandy and stir the sauce until smooth. Cool the sauce to room temperature before serving.

glossy chocolate sauce

makes ²/₃ cup

½ cup superfine sugar

4 tbsp water

6 oz/175 g semisweet chocolate,
  broken into pieces

2 tbsp diced unsalted butter

2 tbsp orange juice

1 Put the sugar and water into a small, heavy-based pan set over low heat and stir until the sugar has dissolved. Stir in the chocolate, a few pieces at a time, waiting until each batch has melted before adding the next. Stir in the butter, a few pieces at a time, waiting until each batch has been incorporated before adding the next. Do not let the sauce boil.

2 Stir in the orange juice and remove the pan from the heat. Serve immediately or keep warm until required. Alternatively, let cool, transfer to a freezerproof container, and freeze for up to 3 months. Thaw at room temperature before re-heating to serve.

french chocolate sauce

makes ⅔ cup

6 tbsp heavy cream

3 oz/85 g semisweet chocolate,
. broken into small pieces

2 tbsp orange-flavored liqueur

1 Bring the cream gently to a boil
in a small, heavy-based pan over
low heat. Remove the pan from the
heat, add the chocolate and stir the
sauce until smooth.

2 Stir in the orange-flavored liqueur
and serve immediately.
Alternatively, if you prefer, keep the
sauce warm until required.

Cold Desserts

Cool, creamy, sumptuous, and indulgent are just a few of the words that spring to mind when you think of cold chocolate desserts. The  desserts contained in this chapter are a combination of all of these.

Some of the desserts are surprisingly quick and simple to make, while others are more elaborate. One of the best things about these desserts is that they can all be made in advance, sometimes days before you need them, making them perfect for entertaining. A quick decoration when necessary is all that is needed on the day. Even the Baked Chocolate Alaska can be assembled in advance and popped into the oven just before serving.

iced white chocolate terrine

serves eight

2 tbsp granulated sugar

5 tbsp water

10½ oz/300 g white chocolate

3 eggs, separated

1¼ cups heavy cream

COOK'S TIP

To make a coulis, place 8 oz/ 225 g soft fruit of your choice, such as strawberries or mangoes in a food processor. Add 1–2 tablespoons of confectioners' sugar and blend. If the fruit contains seeds, push the mixture through a strainer. Serve chilled.

1 Line a 1-lb/450-g loaf pan with foil or plastic wrap, pressing out as many creases as you can. Set the prepared loaf pan aside.

2 Place the granulated sugar and water in a heavy-based pan and heat gently, stirring until the sugar has dissolved. Bring to a boil, then boil for 1–2 minutes until syrupy. Remove the pan from the heat.

3 Break the white chocolate into small pieces and stir it into the syrup, continuing to stir until the chocolate has melted and combined with the syrup. Let cool slightly.

4 Beat the egg yolks into the chocolate mixture. Set aside to cool completely.

5 Lightly whip the cream until just holding its shape, and fold it into the chocolate mixture.

6 Whisk the egg whites in a clean bowl until they are standing in soft peaks. Fold the whites into the chocolate mixture. Pour into the prepared loaf pan and freeze overnight.

7 To serve, remove the terrine from the freezer about 10–15 minutes before serving. Turn out of the pan, cut into slices to serve.

banana coconut cheesecake

serves ten

8 oz/225 g chocolate chip cookies

4 tbsp butter

12 oz/350 g medium-fat soft cheese

⅓ cup superfine sugar

1¾ oz/50 g fresh coconut, grated

2 tbsp coconut-flavored liqueur

2 ripe bananas

4½ oz/125 g semisweet chocolate

1 envelope powdered gelatin

3 tbsp water

⅔ cup heavy cream

TO DECORATE

1 banana

lemon juice

a little melted chocolate

COOK'S TIP

To crack the coconut, carefully pierce 2 of the "eyes" and drain off all the liquid. Tap hard around the center of the coconut with a hammer until it cracks and lever it apart. Cut into slices or grate the flesh.

1 Place the cookies in a plastic bag and crush with a rolling pin. Pour into a mixing bowl. Melt the butter and stir into the cookie crumbs until well coated. Firmly press the cookie mixture into the bottom and up the sides of an 8-inch/20-cm springform cake pan.

2 Beat the soft cheese and superfine sugar together until well combined, then beat in the grated coconut and coconut-flavored liqueur. Mash the 2 bananas and beat them in. Melt the semisweet chocolate and beat in until well combined.

3 Sprinkle the gelatin over the water in a heatproof bowl and let it go spongy. Place over a pan of hot water and stir until dissolved. Stir into the chocolate mixture. Whip the cream until just holding its shape and stir into the chocolate mixture. Spoon the filling over the biscuit shell and let chill for 2 hours, until set.

4 To serve, carefully transfer to a serving plate. Slice the banana, toss in the lemon juice, and arrange around the edge of the cheesecake. Drizzle with melted chocolate and let set before serving.

chocolate rum pots

serves six

8 oz/225 g semisweet chocolate

4 eggs, separated

⅓ cup superfine sugar

4 tbsp dark rum

4 tbsp heavy cream

TO DECORATE

a little whipped cream (optional)

marbled chocolate shapes
    (see page 140)

1 Melt the semisweet chocolate and let cool slightly (see page 6).

2 Whisk the egg yolks with the superfine sugar in a bowl until very pale and fluffy.

3 Drizzle the chocolate into the egg yolk and sugar mixture and fold in together with the dark rum and the heavy cream.

4 Whisk the egg whites in a clean bowl until standing in soft peaks. Fold the egg whites into the chocolate mixture in 2 batches. Divide the mixture between 6 individual dishes, and let chill for at least 2 hours before serving.

5 To serve, decorate with a little whipped cream if wished and a marbled chocolate shape.

chocolate hazelnut pots

serves six

2 eggs

2 egg yolks

1 tbsp superfine sugar

1 tsp cornstarch

2½ cups milk

3 oz/85 g semisweet chocolate

4 tbsp chocolate hazelnut spread

TO DECORATE

grated chocolate or quick chocolate

    curls (see page 7)

1 Beat the eggs, egg yolks, superfine sugar, and cornstarch together until well combined. Heat the milk until it is almost boiling.

2 Gradually pour the milk onto the eggs, whisking as you do so. Melt the chocolate and hazelnut spread in a bowl set over a pan of gently simmering water, then whisk the melted chocolate mixture into the eggs.

3 Pour into 6 small ovenproof dishes and cover the dishes with foil. Place them in a roasting pan. Fill the pan with boiling water until halfway up the sides of the dishes.

4 Bake in a preheated oven, 325°F/160°C, for 35–40 minutes, until the custard is just set. Remove from the pan and cool, then chill until required. Serve decorated with grated chocolate or chocolate curls.

chocolate cheese pots

serves four

1¼ cups ricotta cheese, drained

⅔ cup lowfat unsweetened yogurt

2 tbsp confectioners' sugar

4 tsp lowfat drinking chocolate
   powder

4 tsp unsweetened cocoa

1 tsp vanilla extract

2 tbsp dark rum, optional

2 medium egg whites

4 chocolate cake decorations (see
   page 12)

TO SERVE

pieces of kiwifruit, orange, and
   banana

strawberries and raspberries

1 Mix the ricotta cheese and lowfat yogurt together in a bowl. Sift in the sugar, drinking chocolate, and cocoa and mix well.

2 Add the vanilla extract, and dark rum (if using).

3 Whisk the egg whites in another bowl, until stiff. Using a metal spoon, carefully fold the egg whites into the chocolate mixture.

4 Spoon the yogurt and chocolate mixture into 4 small china dessert pots or ramekins and let chill in the refrigerator for about 30 minutes.

5 Decorate each chocolate cheese pot with a chocolate cake decoration and serve with an assortment of fresh fruit, such as pieces of kiwifruit, orange, and banana, and a few whole strawberries and raspberries or other fruit of your choice.

quick chocolate desserts

serves four

½ cup water

4 tbsp superfine sugar

6 oz/175 g semisweet chocolate,

broken into pieces

3 egg yolks

1¼ cups heavy cream

sweet cookies, to serve

1 Pour the water into a pan and add the sugar. Stir over low heat until the sugar has dissolved. Bring to a boil and continue to boil, without stirring, for 3 minutes. Remove the pan from the heat and let cool slightly.

2 Put the chocolate in a food processor and add the hot syrup. Process until the chocolate has melted, then add the egg yolks and process briefly until smooth. Finally, add the cream to the mixture and process until fully incorporated.

3 Pour the mixture into 4 glasses or individual bowls, cover with plastic wrap, and let chill in the refrigerator for 2 hours, until set. Serve with sweet cookies of your choice.

champagne mousse

SPONGE

4 eggs

½ cup superfine sugar

⅔ cup self-rising flour

2 tbsp unsweetened cocoa

2 tbsp butter, melted

MOUSSE

1 envelope powdered gelatin

3 tbsp water

1¼ cups champagne

1¼ cups heavy cream

2 egg whites

⅓ cup superfine sugar

TO DECORATE

2 oz/50 g semisweet chocolate-
flavored cake covering, melted

1 Line a 15 x 10-inch/38 x 25-cm jelly roll pan with greased baking parchment. Place the eggs and sugar in a bowl and beat, using an electric mixer if you have one, until the mixture is very thick and the whisk leaves a trail when lifted. If using a balloon whisk, stand the bowl over a pan of hot water while whisking. Strain the flour and cocoa together and fold into the egg mixture. Fold in the butter. Pour into the pan and bake in a preheated oven, 400°F/200°C, for 8 minutes or until springy to the touch. Let cool for 5 minutes, then turn out onto a wire rack until cold. Meanwhile, line four 4-inch/10-cm baking rings with baking parchment. Line the sides with 1-inch/2.5-cm strips of cake and the bottom with circles.

2 For the mousse, sprinkle the gelatin over the water and let it go spongy. Place the bowl over a pan of hot water and stir until the gelatin has dissolved. Stir in the champagne.

3 Whip the cream until just holding its shape. Fold in the champagne mixture. Stand in a cool place until on the point of setting, stirring. Whisk the egg whites until standing in soft peaks, add the sugar and whisk until glossy. Carefully fold the egg whites into the setting mixture. Spoon into the sponge cases, allowing the mixture to go above the sponge. Let chill for 2 hours. Pipe the cake covering in squiggles on a piece of parchment, let them set, then use the set squiggles to decorate the mousses.

black forest trifle

serves six

6 thin slices chocolate butter cream
   jelly roll

1 lb 12 oz/800 g canned black
   cherries

2 tbsp kirsch

1 tbsp cornstarch

2 tbsp superfine sugar

generous 1¾ cups milk

3 egg yolks

1 egg

2¾ oz/75 g semisweet chocolate

1¼ cups heavy cream, whipped
   lightly

TO DECORATE

chocolate caraque (see page 7)

maraschino cherries (optional)

1 Place the slices of chocolate jelly roll in the bottom of a glass serving bowl.

2 Drain the black cherries, reserving 6 tablespoons of the juice. Place the cherries and the reserved juice on top of the cake. Sprinkle the kirsch over the black cherries. Set aside.

3 Mix the cornstarch and superfine sugar in a bowl. Stir in enough of the milk to mix to a smooth paste. Beat in the egg yolks and the whole egg.

4 Heat the remaining milk in a small pan until almost boiling, then gradually pour it onto the egg mixture, whisking well until it is combined.

5 Place the bowl over a pan of hot water and cook over low heat until the custard thickens, stirring. Add the chocolate and stir until melted.

6 Pour the chocolate custard over the cherries and cool. When cold, spread the cream over the custard, swirling with the back of a spoon. Let chill before decorating.

7 Decorate with chocolate caraque and whole maraschino cherries, (if using) before serving.

chocolate marquise

serves six

7 oz/200 g semisweet chocolate

generous ⅓ cup butter

3 egg yolks

⅓ cup superfine sugar

1 tsp chocolate extract or 1 tbsp
chocolate-flavored liqueur

1¼ cups heavy cream

TO SERVE

crème fraîche

chocolate-dipped fruits (see page 54)

unsweetened cocoa, for dusting

1 Break the chocolate into pieces. Place the chocolate and butter in a bowl set over a pan of gently simmering water and stir until melted and well combined. Remove the pan from the heat and let the chocolate cool.

2 Place the egg yolks in a mixing bowl with the sugar and whisk until pale and fluffy. Using an electric mixer running on low speed, slowly whisk in the cool chocolate mixture. Stir in the chocolate extract or chocolate-flavored liqueur.

3 Whip the cream until just holding its shape. Fold into the chocolate mixture. Spoon into 6 small custard pots or individual metal molds. Chill the desserts for at least 2 hours.

4 To serve, turn out the desserts onto individual serving dishes. If you have difficulty turning them out, dip the pots or molds into a bowl of warm water for a few seconds to help the marquise to slip out. Serve with chocolate-dipped fruit and crème fraîche and dust with cocoa.

chocolate mint swirl

serves six

1¼ cups heavy cream

⅔ cup mascarpone cheese

2 tbsp confectioners' sugar

1 tbsp crème de menthe

6 oz/175 g semisweet chocolate

semisweet chocolate, to decorate

COOK'S TIP

Pipe the patterns freehand or draw patterns onto baking parchment first, turn the parchment over, and then pipe the chocolate, following the drawn outline.

1 Place the cream in a large mixing bowl and whip it until standing in soft peaks.

2 Fold in the mascarpone cheese and confectioners' sugar, then place about one-third of the mixture in a smaller bowl. Stir the crème de menthe into the smaller bowl. Melt the semisweet chocolate and stir it into the remaining mixture.

3 Place alternate spoonfuls of the 2 mixtures into serving glasses, then swirl the mixture together, using a spoon or knife, to give a decorative two-color effect. Chill until required.

4 To make the piped chocolate decorations, melt a small amount of semisweet chocolate and place in a paper pastry bag.

5 Place a sheet of baking parchment on a board and pipe squiggles, stars, or flower shapes with the melted chocolate. Alternatively, to make curved decorations, pipe decorations onto a long strip of baking parchment, then carefully place the strip over a rolling pin, securing with sticky tape. Let the chocolate set, then carefully remove from the baking parchment.

6 Decorate each dessert with the piped chocolate decorations and serve. The desserts can be decorated and then chilled, if preferred.

121

chocolate banana sundae

serves four

GLOSSY CHOCOLATE SAUCE

2 oz/55 g semisweet chocolate

4 tbsp light corn syrup

1 tbsp butter

1 tbsp brandy or rum, optional

SUNDAE

4 bananas

⅔ cup heavy cream

8–12 scoops good-quality vanilla
    ice cream

¾ cup slivered or chopped almonds,
    toasted

grated chocolate, for sprinkling

4 fan wafer cookies, to serve

1 To make the chocolate sauce, break the chocolate into small pieces and place in a heatproof bowl with the syrup and butter. Heat over a pan of hot water until melted, stirring until well combined. Remove from the heat and stir in the brandy (if using).

2 Slice the bananas and whip the cream until just holding its shape. Place a scoop of ice cream in the bottom of 4 tall sundae dishes. Top with slices of banana, some chocolate sauce, a spoonful of cream, and a good sprinkling of nuts.

3 Repeat the ice cream, banana, and chocolate sauce layers, finishing with a good dollop of whipped cream, sprinkled with nuts, and a little grated chocolate. Serve the chocolate banana sundaes with fan wafer cookies.

white chocolate ice cream

serves six

ICE CREAM

1 egg, plus 1 extra egg yolk

3 tbsp superfine sugar

5½ oz/150 g white chocolate

1¼ cups milk

⅔ cup heavy cream

COOKIE CUPS

1 egg white

4 tbsp superfine sugar

2 tbsp all-purpose flour, sifted

2 tbsp unsweetened cocoa, sifted

2 tbsp butter, melted

semisweet chocolate, melted, to
decorate

1 Place baking parchment on 2 cookie sheets. To make the ice cream, beat the egg, egg yolk, and sugar. Break the chocolate into pieces, place in a bowl with 3 tablespoons of milk, and melt over a pan of hot water. Heat the milk until almost boiling and pour onto the eggs, whisking. Place over a pan of simmering water and stir until the mixture thickens. Whisk in the chocolate. Cover with dampened baking parchment and let cool.

2 Whip the cream and fold into the custard. Transfer to a freezer proof container and freeze the mixture for 1–2 hours. Scrape into a bowl and beat until smooth. Re-freeze until firm.

3 Beat the egg white and sugar. Beat in the flour and cocoa, then the butter. Place 1 tablespoon on 1 cookie sheet and spread out into a 5-inch/12.5-cm circle. Bake in a preheated oven, 400°F/200°C, for 4–5 minutes. Remove and mold over an upturned cup. Let set, then cool. Repeat to make 6 cookie cups. Serve the ice cream in the cups, drizzled with melted chocolate.

marble cheesecake

serves ten

BASE

8 oz/225 g toasted oat cereal

½ cup toasted hazelnuts, chopped

4 tbsp butter

1 oz/25 g semisweet chocolate

FILLING

12 oz/350 g full-fat soft cheese

½ cup superfine sugar

generous ¼ cup thick yogurt

1¼ cups heavy cream

1 envelope powdered gelatin

3 tbsp water

6 oz/175 g semisweet chocolate,
   melted

6 oz/175 g white chocolate, melted

1 Place the toasted oat cereal in a plastic bag and crush it coarsely with a rolling pin. Pour the crushed cereal into a mixing bowl and stir in the toasted chopped hazelnuts.

2 Melt the butter and chocolate together over low heat and stir into the cereal mixture, stirring until well coated.

3 Using the bottom of a glass, press the mixture into the bottom and up the sides of an 8-inch/20-cm springform cake pan.

4 Beat the cheese and sugar together with a wooden spoon until smooth. Beat in the yogurt. Whip the cream until just holding its shape and fold into the mixture. Sprinkle the gelatin over the water in a heatproof bowl and let it go spongy. Place over a pan of hot water and stir until dissolved. Stir into the mixture.

5 Divide the mixture in half and beat the semisweet chocolate into one half and the white chocolate into the other half.

6 Place alternate spoonfuls of mixture on top of the cereal base. Swirl the filling together with the tip of a knife to give a marbled effect. Smooth the top with a scraper or a spatula. Chill the cheesecake for at least 2 hours, until set, before serving.

chocolate fruit tartlets

serves six

2¼ cups all-purpose flour

3 tbsp unsweetened cocoa

⅔ cup butter

3 tbsp superfine sugar

2–3 tbsp water

1¾ oz/50 g semisweet chocolate

½ cup chopped mixed nuts, toasted

12 oz/350 g prepared fruit

3 tbsp apricot jelly or red currant
jelly

VARIATION

If liked, you can fill the cases
with a little sweetened cream
before topping with the fruit.
For a chocolate-flavored filling,
blend 8 oz/225 g chocolate
hazelnut spread with
5 tablespoons of thick yogurt
or whipped cream.

1 Sift the flour and cocoa into a
mixing bowl. Cut the butter into
small pieces and rub into the flour
with your fingertips until the mixture
resembles fine bread crumbs.

2 Stir in the sugar. Add enough
of the water to mix to a soft
dough—about 1–2 tablespoons.
Cover and chill for 15 minutes.

3 Roll out the pie dough on a lightly
floured counter and use to line
6 tartlet pans, each 4 inches/10 cm
across. Prick the shells with a fork and
line with a little crumpled foil. Bake in
a preheated oven, 375°F/190°C, for
10 minutes.

4 Remove the foil and bake for
another 5–10 minutes, until the
pie dough is crisp. Place the pans on
a wire rack to cool completely.

5 Melt the chocolate. Spread
out the toasted chopped mixed
nuts on a plate. Remove the pie
shells from the pans. Spread melted
chocolate on the rims, then dip in the
nuts. Let the chocolate set.

6 Arrange the fruit in the tartlet
shells. Melt the apricot or red
currant jelly with the remaining
tablespoon of water and brush it over
the fruit. Chill the tartlets until required.

chocolate cheesecake

serves twelve

¾ cup all-purpose flour

¾ cup ground almonds

1⅓ cups raw brown sugar

⅔ cup margarine

1½ lb/675 g firm bean curd, drained

¾ cup vegetable oil

½ cup orange juice

¾ cup brandy

½ cup unsweetened cocoa, plus

   extra to decorate

2 tsp almond extract

TO DECORATE

confectioners' sugar

Cape gooseberries

1 Put the flour, ground almonds, and 1 tablespoon of the sugar in a bowl and mix well. Rub the margarine into the mixture to form a dough.

2 Lightly grease and line the bottom of a 9-inch/23-cm springform cake pan. Press the dough into the bottom of the pan to cover, pushing the dough up to the edge of the pan.

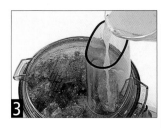

3 Coarsely chop the bean curd and put it in a food processor with the vegetable oil, orange juice, brandy, cocoa, almond essence, and remaining

sugar, and process until smooth and creamy. Pour the mixture evenly over the dough in the pan and smooth out, using a spatula. Cook in a preheated oven, 325°F/160°C, for 1–1¼ hours or until set.

4 Let cool in the pan for 5 minutes, then remove from the pan and chill. Dust with confectioners' sugar and cocoa. Decorate the chocolate cheesecake with Cape gooseberries and serve.

tiramisù layers

serves six

⅔ cup heavy cream

10½ oz/300 g semisweet chocolate

14 oz/400 g mascarpone cheese

1¾ cup black coffee with

⅓ cup superfine sugar, cooled

6 tbsp dark rum or brandy

36 ladyfingers, about 14 oz/400 g

unsweetened cocoa, for dusting

VARIATION

Try adding ⅓ cup toasted, chopped hazelnuts to the chocolate cream mixture in Step 1, if you prefer.

1 Whip the cream until it just holds its shape. Melt the chocolate in a bowl set over a pan of simmering water, stirring occasionally. Let the chocolate cool slightly, then stir it into the mascarpone cheese and cream.

2 Mix the coffee and rum together in a bowl. Dip the ladyfingers into the mixture briefly so that they absorb the coffee and rum mixture but do not become soggy.

3 Place 3 ladyfingers on 3 individual serving plates.

4 Spoon a layer of the chocolate, mascarpone, and cream mixture over the ladyfingers.

5 Place 3 more lady fingers on top of the chocolate and mascarpone mixture. Spread another layer of chocolate and mascarpone and place 3 more ladyfingers on top.

6 Let the tiramisù chill in the refrigerator for at least 1 hour. Dust the dessert with unsweetened cocoa just before serving.

strawberry cheesecake

serves eight

BASE

¼ cup unsalted butter

2⅔ cups crushed graham crackers

½ cup chopped walnuts

FILLING

2 cups mascarpone cheese

2 eggs, beaten

3 tbsp superfine sugar

9 oz/250 g white chocolate, broken
    into pieces

2 cups strawberries, hulled and
    quartered

TOPPING

¾ cup mascarpone cheese

chocolate caraque (see page 7)

16 whole strawberries

1 Melt the butter over low heat and
stir in the crushed crackers and
the nuts. Spoon the mixture into a
9-inch/23-cm loose-bottomed cake pan
and press evenly over the bottom with
the back of a spoon. Set aside.

2 Preheat the oven to 300°F/150°C.
To make the filling, beat the cheese
until smooth, then beat in the eggs and
sugar. Put the chocolate into the top of a
double boiler or in a heatproof bowl set
over a pan of barely simmering water. Stir
over low heat until melted and smooth.
Remove from the heat and cool slightly,
then stir into the cheese mixture. Finally,
stir in the strawberries.

3 Spoon the mixture into the cake
pan, spread out evenly and
smooth the surface. Bake in a
preheated oven for 1 hour, until the
filling is just firm. Turn off the oven but
and let the cheesecake cool inside it
until completely cold.

4 Transfer the cheesecake to a
serving plate and spread the
mascarpone cheese on top. Decorate
with chocolate caraque and whole
strawberries.

chocolate brandy torte

serves twelve

BASE

9 oz/250 g gingersnaps

2¾ oz/75 g semisweet chocolate

generous ⅓ cup butter

FILLING

8 oz/225 g semisweet chocolate

9 oz/250 g mascarpone cheese

2 eggs, separated

3 tbsp brandy

1¼ cups heavy cream

4 tbsp superfine sugar

TO DECORATE

scant ½ cup heavy cream

chocolate-coated coffee beans

3 Lightly whip the cream until just holding its shape and carefully fold in the chocolate mixture.

4 Whisk the egg whites in a clean bowl until standing in soft peaks. Add the superfine sugar a little at a time and whisk until thick and glossy. Fold into the chocolate mixture, in 2 batches, until just mixed.

5 Spoon into the gingersnap shell and let chill for at least 2 hours. Transfer to a serving plate. Whip the cream and pipe rosettes onto the cheesecake, then add the chocolate-coated coffee beans.

1 Crush the gingersnaps in a plastic bag with a rolling pin or in a food processor. Melt the chocolate and butter together and pour over the gingersnaps. Mix well, then use to line the bottom and sides of a 9-inch/23-cm loose-bottomed fluted flan pan. Chill while preparing the filling.

2 To make the filling, melt the chocolate in a pan, remove from the heat, and beat in the mascarpone cheese, egg yolks, and brandy.

rich chocolate ice cream

1 Beat the egg, egg yolks, and superfine sugar together in a mixing bowl until well combined. Heat the milk until it is almost boiling.

2 Gradually pour the hot milk onto the eggs, whisking as you do so. Place the bowl over a pan of gently simmering water and cook, stirring constantly, until the custard mixture thickens sufficiently to thinly coat the back of a wooden spoon.

3 Break the semisweet chocolate into small pieces and add to the hot custard. Stir until has melted. Cover with a sheet of dampened baking parchment and let cool.

4 Whip the cream until just holding its shape, then fold into the cooled chocolate custard. Transfer to a freezer proof container and freeze for 1–2 hours until the mixture is frozen 1 inch/2.5 cm from the sides.

5 Scrape the ice cream into a chilled bowl and beat again until smooth. Re-freeze until firm.

6 To make the trellis cups, invert a muffin pan and cover 6 alternate mounds with plastic wrap. Melt the chocolate, place it in a paper pastry bag, and snip off the end.

7 Pipe a circle around the bottom of the mound, then pipe chocolate back and forth over it to form a trellis; carefully pipe a double thickness. Pipe around the bottom again. Chill until set, then lift from the pan and remove the plastic wrap. Serve the chocolate ice cream in the trellis cups.

chocolate freezer cake

serves eight

4 eggs

¾ cup superfine sugar

¾ cup self-rising flour

scant ⅓ cup unsweetened cocoa

2¼ cups chocolate and mint ice
cream

Glossy Chocolate Sauce (see
page 104)

1 Lightly grease a 9-inch/23-cm ring
pan. Place the eggs and sugar in
a large mixing bowl. Using an electric
mixer if you have one, whisk the
mixture until it is very thick and the
whisk leaves a trail. If using a balloon
whisk, stand the bowl over a pan of
hot water while whisking.

2 Sift the flour and cocoa together
and fold into the egg mixture.
Pour into the prepared pan and bake in
a preheated oven, 350°F/180°C, for
30 minutes or until springy to the
touch. Let cool in the pan before
turning out on to a wire rack to cool
completely.

3 Rinse the cake pan and line
with a strip of plastic wrap,
overhanging slightly. Carefully cut off
the top ½ inch/1 cm of the cake in one
slice, and then set aside.

4 Return the cake to the pan. Using
a spoon, scoop out the center of
the cake, leaving a shell about
1-cm/½-inch thick.

5 Remove the ice cream from the
freezer and let stand for a few
minutes, then beat with a wooden
spoon until softened a little. Fill the
center of the cake with the ice cream,
carefully smoothing the top. Replace
the top of the cake.

6 Cover with the overhanging
plastic wrap and freeze the cake
for at least 2 hours.

7 To serve, turn the chocolate
freezer cake out onto a serving
dish and drizzle over some of the
Chocolate Sauce in an attractive
pattern, if wished. Cut the cake into
slices and then serve the remaining
chocolate sauce separately.

chocolate mousse

serves eight

3½ oz/100 g semisweet chocolate, melted

1¼ cups unsweetened yogurt

⅔ cup Quark

4 tbsp superfine sugar

1 tbsp orange juice

1 tbsp brandy

1½ tsp gelozone (vegetarian gelatin)

9 tbsp cold water

2 large egg whites

coarsely grated semisweet and white chocolate and orange rind, to decorate

1 Put the melted chocolate, yogurt, Quark, sugar, orange juice, and brandy in a food processor and process for 30 seconds. Transfer the mixture to a large bowl.

2 Sprinkle the gelozone over the water and stir until dissolved.

3 Put the gelozone and water in a pan and boil for 2 minutes. Cool slightly, then stir into the chocolate.

4 Whisk the egg whites until stiff peaks form and fold into the chocolate mixture using a metal spoon.

5 Line a 1 lb 2-oz/500-g loaf pan with plastic wrap. Spoon the mousse into the pan. Chill in the refrigerator for 2 hours, until set. Turn the mousse out onto a serving plate and decorate with grated chocolate and orange rind.

chocolate charlotte

serves eight

about 22 ladyfingers

4 tbsp orange-flavored liqueur

9 oz/250 g semisweet chocolate

⅔ cup heavy cream

4 eggs

⅔ cup superfine sugar

TO DECORATE

⅔ cup whipping cream

2 tbsp superfine sugar

½ tsp vanilla extract

quick semisweet chocolate curls (see page 7)

chocolate decorations (see page 121), optional

1 Line the bottom of a Charlotte mold or a deep 7-inch/18-cm round cake pan.

2 Place the ladyfingers on a tray and sprinkle with half of the orange-flavored liqueur. Use to line the sides of the mold or pan, trimming if necessary to make a tight fit.

3 Break the chocolate into small pieces, place in a bowl and melt over a pan of hot water. Remove from the heat and stir in the heavy cream.

4 Separate the eggs and place the whites in a large clean bowl. Set aside. Beat the egg yolks into the chocolate and cream mixture.

5 Whisk the egg whites until standing in stiff peaks, then gradually add the superfine sugar, whisking until stiff and glossy. Carefully fold the egg whites into the chocolate mixture in 2 batches, taking care not to knock out all of the air. Pour into the center of the mold. Trim the ladyfingers so that they are level with the chocolate mixture. Chill the chocolate charlotte in the refrigerator for at least 5 hours before decorating and serving.

6 To decorate, whip the cream, sugar, and vanilla extract until standing in soft peaks. Turn out the Charlotte onto a serving plate. Pipe cream rosettes around the bottom and decorate with chocolate curls and other decorations of your choice.

mocha swirl mousse

serves four

1 tbsp coffee and chicory extract

2 tsp unsweetened cocoa, plus extra
   for dusting

1 tsp low-fat drinking chocolate
   powder

²∕₃ cup lowfat crème fraîche, plus
   4 tsp to serve

2 tsp powdered gelatin

2 tbsp boiling water

2 large egg whites

2 tbsp superfine sugar

4 chocolate-coated coffee beans,
   to serve

1 Place the coffee and chicory extract in one bowl, and 2 teaspoons of cocoa and the drinking chocolate in another bowl. Divide the crème fraîche between the 2 bowls and mix both well.

2 Dissolve the gelatin in the boiling water and set aside. Whisk the egg whites and sugar in a clean bowl, until stiff and divide this evenly between the 2 mixtures.

3 Divide the dissolved gelatin between the 2 mixtures and, using a large metal spoon, gently fold until well mixed.

4 Spoon small amounts of the 2 mousses alternately into 4 serving glasses and swirl together gently. Chill for 1 hour or until set.

5 To serve, top each mousse with a teaspoon of crème fraîche, a chocolate coffee bean, and a light dusting of cocoa. Serve immediately.

layered chocolate mousse

serves four

3 eggs

1 tsp cornstarch

4 tbsp superfine sugar

1¼ cups milk

1 envelope powdered gelatin

3 tbsp water

1¼ cups heavy cream

2¾ oz/75 g semisweet chocolate

2¾ oz/75 g white chocolate

2¾ oz/75 g light chocolate

chocolate caraque, to decorate (see page 7)

1 Line a 1-lb/450-g loaf pan with baking parchment. Separate the eggs, putting each egg white in a separate bowl. Place the egg yolks, cornstarch, and sugar in a large mixing bowl and whisk until well combined. Place the milk in a pan and heat gently, stirring until almost boiling. Pour the milk onto the egg yolks, whisking.

2 Set the bowl over a pan of gently simmering water and cook, stirring until the mixture thickens enough to thinly coat the back of a wooden spoon.

3 Sprinkle the gelatin over the water in a small heatproof bowl and let it go spongy. Place over a pan of hot water and stir until dissolved. Stir into the hot mixture. Let the mixture cool.

4 Whip the cream until just holding its shape. Fold into the egg custard, then divide the mixture into 3. Melt the 3 types of chocolate separately. Fold the semisweet chocolate into one egg custard portion. Whisk one egg white until standing in soft peaks and fold into the semisweet chocolate custard until combined. Pour

into the prepared pan and smooth the top. Chill in the refrigerator until just set. The remaining mixtures should stay at room temperature.

5 Fold the white chocolate into another portion of the egg custard. Whisk another egg white and fold in. Pour on top of the semisweet chocolate layer and chill quickly. Repeat with the remaining light chocolate and egg white. Chill for at least 2 hours, until set. Turn out onto a serving dish and decorate with chocolate caraque.

chocolate & vanilla creams

serves four

scant 2 cups heavy cream

⅓ cup superfine sugar

1 vanilla bean

generous ¾ cup crème fraîche

2 tsp powdered gelatin

3 tbsp water

1¾ oz/50 g semisweet chocolate

MARBLED CHOCOLATE SHAPES

a little melted white chocolate

a little melted semisweet chocolate

1 Place the cream and sugar in a pan. Cut the vanilla bean into 2 pieces and add to the cream. Heat gently, stirring until the sugar has dissolved, then bring to a boil. Lower the heat and let simmer for 2–3 minutes.

2 Remove the pan from the heat and take out the vanilla bean. Stir in the crème fraîche.

3 Sprinkle the gelatin over the water in a small heatproof bowl and let it go spongy, then place over a pan of hot water and stir until dissolved. Stir the gelatin into the cream mixture. Pour half of this mixture into another mixing bowl.

4 Melt the semisweet chocolate and stir it into one half of the cream mixture. Pour the chocolate mixture into 4 individual glass serving dishes and chill for 15–20 minutes until just set. While the chocolate mixture is chilling, keep the vanilla mixture at room temperature.

5 Take the serving dishes out of the refrigerator spoon the vanilla mixture on top of the chocolate mixture and chill again until the vanilla is set.

6 Meanwhile, make the shapes for the decoration. Spoon the melted white chocolate into a paper pastry bag and snip off the tip. Spread some melted semisweet chocolate on a piece of baking parchment. While still wet, pipe a fine line of white chocolate in a scribble over the top. Use the tip of a toothpick to marble the white chocolate into the semisweet. When firm but not too hard, carefully cut into shapes with a small shaped cutter or a sharp knife. Chill the marbled chocolate shapes until firm, then use to decorate the desserts.

raspberry chocolate boxes

serves twelve

7 oz/200 g semisweet chocolate,
    broken into pieces

1½ tsp cold, strong black coffee

1 egg yolk

1½ tsp coffee liqueur

2 egg whites

7 oz/200g raspberries

SPONGE CAKE

1 egg, plus 1 egg white

¼ cup superfine sugar

scant ½ cup all-purpose flour

1 To make the mocha mousse, melt 2 oz/55 g of the chocolate in a heatproof bowl set over a pan of barely simmering water. Add the coffee and stir over low heat until smooth, then remove from the heat and let cool slightly. Stir in the egg yolk and the coffee liqueur.

2 Whisk the egg whites into stiff peaks. Fold into the chocolate mixture, cover with plastic wrap, and let chill for 2 hours, until set.

3 For the sponge cake, lightly grease an 8-inch/20-cm square cake pan and line the bottom with baking parchment. Put the egg and extra white with the sugar in a heatproof bowl set over a pan of barely simmering water. Whisk over low heat for 5–10 minutes, until pale and thick. Remove from the heat and continue whisking for 10 minutes, until cold and the whisk leaves a ribbon trail when lifted.

4 Preheat the oven to 350°F/180°C. Sift the flour over the egg mixture and gently fold it in. Pour into the prepared pan. Bake in the preheated oven for 20–25 minutes, until firm. Turn out onto a wire rack to cool, then invert the cake, keeping the baking parchment in place.

5 To make the chocolate boxes, grease a 12 x 9-inch/30 x 23-cm jelly roll pan and line with waxed paper. Place the remaining chocolate in a heatproof bowl set over a pan of barely simmering water. Stir over low heat until melted, but not too runny. Pour it into the pan and spread evenly with a spatula. Set aside in a cool place for about 30 minutes, until set.

6 Turn out the set chocolate, cut it into 36 rectangles, measuring 3 x 1 inches/7.5 x 2.5 cm. Cut 12 of these in half to make 24 rectangles measuring 1½ x 1 inches/4 x 2.5 cm.

7 Trim the sponge cake, then cut into 12 slices, measuring 3 x 1¼ inches/7.5 x 3 cm. Spread a little of the mousse along the sides of each sponge rectangle and press 2 long and 2 short chocolate rectangles on each side to make boxes. Divide the remaining mousse among the boxes and top with the raspberries.

mocha creams

serves four

8 oz/225 g semisweet chocolate

1 tbsp instant coffee powder

1¼ cups boiling water

1 envelope powdered gelatin

3 tbsp cold water

1 tsp vanilla extract

1 tbsp coffee-flavored liqueur,
optional

1¼ cups heavy cream

4 chocolate-coated coffee beans

8 amaretti cookies

VARIATION

To add a delicious almond
flavor to the dessert, replace
the coffee-flavored liqueur
with Amaretto liqueur.

3 Stir in the vanilla extract and coffee-flavored liqueur (if using). Let the chocolate mixture stand in a cool place until just starting to thicken. Whisk from time to time.

4 Whisk the cream until it is standing in soft peaks, then set aside a little for decorating the desserts and fold the remainder into the chocolate mixture. Spoon the mixture into tall glass serving dishes and let set.

5 Decorate with the reserved cream and chocolate coffee beans and serve with the amaretti cookies.

1 Break the chocolate into small pieces and place in a pan with the coffee. Stir in the boiling water and heat gently, stirring until the chocolate melts.

2 Sprinkle the gelatin over the cold water and let it go spongy, then whisk it into the hot chocolate mixture to dissolve it.

banana cream profiteroles

serves four

DOUGH

⅔ cup water

5 tbsp butter

¾ cup strong all-purpose flour, sifted

2 eggs

CHOCOLATE SAUCE

3½ oz/100 g semisweet chocolate, broken into pieces

2 tbsp water

4 tbsp confectioners' sugar

2 tbsp sweet butter

FILLING

1¼ cups heavy cream

1 banana

2 tbsp confectioners' sugar

2 tbsp banana-flavored liqueur

1 Lightly grease a cookie sheet and sprinkle with a little water. To make the choux pastry dough, place the water in a pan. Cut the butter into small pieces and add to the pan. Heat gently until the butter melts, then bring to a rolling boil. Remove the pan from the heat and add the flour in one go, beating well until the mixture leaves the sides of the pan and forms a ball. Let cool slightly, then gradually beat in the eggs to form a smooth, glossy mixture. Spoon the choux pastry dough into a large pastry bag fitted with a ½-inch/1-cm plain tip.

2 Pipe about 18 small balls of the dough onto the cookie sheet, allowing enough room for them to expand during cooking. Bake in a preheated oven, 425°F/220°C, for 15–20 minutes, until crisp and golden. Remove from the oven and, using a sharp knife, make a small slit in each one for steam to escape. Cool the profiteroles on a wire rack.

3 To make the chocolate sauce, place all the ingredients in a heatproof bowl set over a pan of simmering water, and heat until combined to make a smooth, glossy sauce, stirring constantly.

4 To make the filling, whip the cream until standing in soft peaks. Mash the banana with the sugar and liqueur. Fold into the cream. Place in a pastry bag fitted with a ½-inch/1-cm plain tip and pipe into the profiteroles. Serve the profiteroles mounded up on a glass cake stand, with the sauce poured over.

cardamom cream horns

serves six

1 egg white

4 tbsp superfine sugar

2 tbsp all-purpose flour

2 tbsp unsweetened cocoa

2 tbsp butter, melted

1¾ oz/50 g semisweet chocolate

CARDAMOM CREAM

⅔ cup heavy cream

1 tbsp confectioners' sugar

¼ tsp ground cardamom

pinch of ground ginger

1 oz/25 g preserved ginger, chopped finely

1 Place a sheet of baking parchment on 2 cookie sheets. Lightly grease 6 cream horn molds. To make the horns, beat the egg white and sugar in a mixing bowl until well combined. Sift the flour and cocoa together, then beat into the egg white and sugar mixture followed by the melted butter.

2 Bake 1 chocolate cone at a time. Place 1 tablespoon of the mixture onto 1 cookie sheet and spread out to form a 5-inch/13-cm circle. Bake in a preheated oven, 400°F/200°C, for 4–5 minutes.

3 Working quickly, remove the cookie with a spatula and wrap around the cream horn mold to form a cone. Let the cone set, then remove from the mold. Repeat with the remaining mixture to make 6 cones.

4 Melt the chocolate and dip the open edges of the horn in the chocolate. Place on a piece of baking parchment and let the chocolate set.

5 To make the cardamom cream, place the cream in a bowl and sift the confectioners' sugar and ground spices over the surface. Whisk the heavy cream until standing in soft peaks. Fold in the chopped preserved ginger and use the mixture to fill the chocolate cones.

chocolate shortcake towers

serves six

1 cup butter

½ cup brown sugar

1¾ oz/50 g semisweet chocolate

scant 2½ cups all-purpose flour

COULIS

12 oz/350 g fresh raspberries

2 tbsp confectioners' sugar

WHITE CHOCOLATE CREAM

1¼ cups heavy cream

3 tbsp milk

3½ oz/100 g white chocolate,
   melted

confectioners' sugar, for dusting

1 Lightly grease a cookie sheet.
Beat the butter and sugar
together until light and fluffy. Grate the
chocolate and beat it into the mixture.
Mix in the all-purpose flour to form a
stiff dough.

2 Roll out the dough on a lightly
floured counter and stamp out
18 circles, 3 inches/7.5 cm across, with
a fluted cookie cutter. Place the circles
on the cookie sheet and bake in a
preheated oven, 400°F/200°C, for
10 minutes, until they are crisp and
golden. Let the shortcake circles cool
on the sheet.

3 To make the coulis, set aside about
3½ oz/100 g of the raspberries.
Blend the remainder in a food processor
with the confectioners' sugar, then
push through a strainer to remove the
seeds. Chill. Set aside 2 teaspoons of
the cream. Whip the remainder until
just holding its shape. Fold in the milk
and the melted chocolate.

4 For each tower, spoon a little
coulis onto a serving plate. Drop
small dots of the reserved cream into
the coulis around the edge of the plate
and use a toothpick to drag through the
cream to make an attractive pattern.

5 Place a shortcake circle on the
plate and spoon on a little of
the chocolate cream. Top with 2 or
3 raspberries, top with another shortcake, and repeat. Place a third biscuit
on top. Dust with sugar to serve.

baked chocolate alaska

serves four

2 eggs

4 tbsp superfine sugar

¼ cup all-purpose flour

2 tbsp unsweetened cocoa

3 egg whites

⅔ cup superfine sugar

4 cups good-quality chocolate ice
cream

1 Grease a 7-inch/18-cm round
cake pan and line the bottom
with baking parchment.

2 Whisk the eggs and the
4 tablespoons of sugar in a
mixing bowl until very thick and pale.
Sift the flour and cocoa together and
carefully fold in.

3 Pour into the prepared pan
and bake in a preheated oven,
425°F/220°C, for 7 minutes or until
springy to the touch. Transfer to a
wire rack to cool completely.

4 Whisk the egg whites in a clean
bowl until they are standing in
soft peaks. Gradually add the superfine
sugar, whisking until you have a thick,
glossy meringue.

5 Place the sponge on a cookie
sheet and pile the ice cream onto
the center in a heaped dome.

COOK'S TIP

This dessert is delicious served
with a black currant coulis. Cook
a few black currants in a little
orange juice until soft, blend to a
purée and push through a
strainer, then sweeten to taste
with a little confectioners' sugar.

6 Pipe or spread the meringue
over the ice cream, making sure
the ice cream is completely enclosed.
(At this point the dessert can be
frozen, if wished.)

7 Return the dessert to the oven, for
5 minutes, until the meringue is
just golden. Serve immediately.

chocolate orange sherbet

serves four

2 tsp vegetable oil, for brushing

8 oz/225 g semisweet chocolate,
    broken into small pieces

4 cups crushed ice

2¼ cups freshly squeezed orange
    juice

⅔ cup water

¼ cup superfine sugar

finely grated rind of 1 orange

juice and finely grated rind of
    1 lemon

1 tsp powdered gelatin

3 tbsp orange-flavored liqueur

fresh mint sprigs, to decorate

1 Brush a 3¼-cup mold with oil,
drain well, then chill in the
refrigerator. Put the chocolate in the
top of a double boiler or into a
heatproof bowl set over a pan of
barely simmering water. Stir the
chocolate over low heat until melted,
then remove from the heat.

2 Remove the mold from the
refrigerator and pour in the
melted chocolate. Tip and turn the
mold to coat the interior. Place the
mold on a bed of crushed ice and
continue tipping and turning until the
chocolate has set. Return the mold
to the refrigerator.

3 Set aside 3 tablespoons of the
orange juice in a small, heatproof
bowl. Pour the remainder into a pan
and add the water, sugar, orange rind,
and lemon juice and rind. Stir over low
heat until the sugar has dissolved, then
increase the heat and bring the mixture
to a boil. Remove the pan
from the heat.

4 Sprinkle the gelatin over the
orange juice. Set aside for
2 minutes to soften, then set over a
pan of barely simmering water until
dissolved. Stir the gelatin and the
liqueur into the orange juice mixture.
Pour into a freezerproof container and
freeze for 30 minutes.

5 Remove the sherbet from the
freezer, transfer to a bowl, and
beat thoroughly to break up the ice
crystals. Return it to the container and
freeze for 1 hour. Repeat this process
3 more times.

6 Remove the sherbet from the
freezer, and beat well. Remove
the mold from the refrigerator and
spoon the sherbet into it. Freeze
overnight. When ready to serve,
unmold the sherbet and decorate
with mint.

chocolate & almond tart

serves eight

PIE DOUGH

1¼ cups all-purpose flour

2 tbsp superfine sugar

½ cup butter, cut into small pieces

1 tbsp water

FILLING

½ cup light corn syrup

4 tbsp butter

½ cup soft brown sugar

3 eggs, beaten lightly

½ cup whole blanched almonds,
   chopped coarsely

3½ oz/100 g white chocolate,
   chopped coarsely

cream, to serve (optional)

1 To make the tart shell, place the flour and sugar in a mixing bowl and rub in the butter with your fingertips. Add the water and work the mixture together into a soft dough. Wrap and let chill for 30 minutes.

2 Roll out the dough on a lightly floured counter and use to line a 9½-inch/24-cm loose-bottomed flan pan. Prick the tart shell with a fork and let chill for 30 minutes. Line the shell with foil and baking beans and bake in a preheated oven, 375°F/190°C, for 15 minutes. Remove the foil and baking beans and cook for another 15 minutes.

3 To make the filling, gently melt the syrup, butter, and sugar together in a pan. Remove from the heat and let cool slightly. Stir in the beaten eggs, almonds, and chocolate.

4 Pour the chocolate and nut filling into the prepared tart shell and cook in the oven for 30–35 minutes or until just set. Let cool before removing the tart from the pan. Serve the tart with cream, if wished.

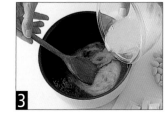

chocolate pear tart

serves eight

DOUGH

scant 1 cup all-purpose flour

pinch of salt

2 tbsp superfine sugar

½ cup diced unsalted butter

1 egg yolk

1 tbsp lemon juice

TOPPING

4 oz/115 g semisweet chocolate,
   grated

4 pears

½ cup light cream

1 egg, plus 1 egg yolk

½ tsp almond extract

3 tbsp superfine sugar

1 To make the dough, sift the flour and a pinch of salt into a mixing bowl. Add the sugar and butter and mix well with a dough blender or 2 forks until thoroughly incorporated. Stir in the egg yolk and the lemon juice to form a dough. Form the dough into a ball, wrap in plastic wrap, and let it chill in the refrigerator for 30 minutes.

2 Roll out the dough on a lightly floured counter and use it to line a 10-inch/25-cm loose-bottomed tart pan. Sprinkle the grated semisweet chocolate over the bottom of the tart shell. Peel the pears, cut them in half lengthwise, and remove the cores. Thinly slice each pear half and fan out slightly. Using a spatula, scoop up each sliced pear half and arrange neatly in the tart shell.

3 Beat the cream, egg, extra yolk, and almond extract together, and spoon the mixture over the pears. Sprinkle the sugar over the tart.

4 Bake in a preheated oven 400°F/200°C for 10 minutes, then lower the temperature to 350°F/180°C and bake for another 20 minutes, until the pears are starting to caramelize and the filling is just set. Remove from the oven. Decorate and serve.

153

chocolate pecan pie

serves ten

PIE DOUGH

2½ cups all-purpose flour

½ cup unsweetened cocoa

1 cup confectioners' sugar

scant 1 cup unsalted butter, diced

1 egg yolk

pinch of salt

FILLING

3 oz/85 g semisweet chocolate,
    broken into small pieces

3 cups shelled pecans

6 tbsp unsalted butter

generous 1 cup brown sugar

3 eggs

2 tbsp heavy cream

¼ cup all-purpose flour

1 tbsp confectioners' sugar, for
    dusting

1 To make the pie dough, sift the flour, cocoa, sugar, and salt into a mixing bowl and make a well in the center. Put the butter and egg yolk in the well and gradually mix in the dry ingredients. Knead lightly into a ball. Cover with plastic wrap and chill in the refrigerator for 1 hour.

2 Unwrap the dough and roll it out on a lightly floured counter. Use the dough to line a 10-inch/25-cm non-stick springform pie pan and prick the shell all over with a fork. Line the pie shell with baking parchment and fill with baking beans. Bake the pie shell in the preheated oven 350°F/180°C for 15 minutes. Remove from the oven, discard the beans and paper, and let the pie shell cool.

3 To make the filling, put the chocolate in a heatproof bowl set over a pan of barely simmering water. Stir until melted. Remove from the heat and set aside. Coarsely chop 2 cups of the pecans and set aside. Mix the butter with ⅓ cup of the brown sugar. Beat in the eggs, one at a time, then add the remaining brown sugar and mix well. Stir in the cream, flour, melted chocolate, and chopped pecans.

4 Spoon into the pie shell. Cut the remaining pecans in half and arrange in concentric circles over the pie.

5 Bake in the preheated oven at the same temperature for 30 minutes, then cover the top with foil. Bake for another 25 minutes. Remove from the pan and transfer to a wire rack to cool completely. Dust with confectioners' sugar and serve.

mississippi mud pie

serves eight

2 cups all-purpose flour

¼ cup unsweetened cocoa

⅔ cup butter

2 tbsp superfine sugar

about 2 tbsp cold water

FILLING

¾ cup butter

2⅓ cups brown sugar

4 eggs, beaten lightly

4 tbsp unsweetened cocoa, sifted

5½ oz/150 g semisweet chocolate

1¼ cups light cream

1 tsp chocolate extract

TO DECORATE

1¾ cups heavy cream, whipped

chocolate flakes and quick chocolate

curls (see page 7)

1 To make the pie dough, sift the flour and cocoa into a mixing bowl. Rub in the butter until the mixture resembles fine bread crumbs. Stir in the sugar and enough cold water to mix to a soft dough. Chill for 15 minutes.

2 Roll out the dough on a lightly floured counter and use to line a deep 9-inch/23-cm loose-bottomed flan pan or ceramic flan dish. Line with foil or baking parchment and baking beans. Bake blind in a preheated oven, 375°F/190°C, for 15 minutes. Remove the beans and foil or parchment and cook the pie shell for another 10 minutes, until it is crisp.

3 To make the filling, beat the butter and sugar in a bowl and gradually beat in the eggs with the cocoa. Melt the chocolate and beat it into the mixture with the light cream and the chocolate extract.

4 Pour the mixture into the cooked pie shell and bake at 325°F/160°C, for 45 minutes or until the filling is set.

5 Let the mud pie cool completely, then transfer the pie to a serving plate, if preferred. Cover with the whipped cream and let chill.

6 Decorate the pie with quick chocolate curls and chocolate flakes and then let it chill.

white chocolate molds

serves six

4½ oz/125 g white chocolate,
    broken into pieces

scant 1 cup heavy cream

3 tbsp crème fraîche

2 eggs, separated

3 tbsp water

1½ tsp powdered gelatin

1 cup sliced strawberries

scant 1 cup raspberries

1¼ cups black currants

5 tbsp superfine sugar

½ cup raspberry flavored liqueur

12 black currant leaves, if available

1 Put the chocolate into the top of a double boiler or in a heatproof bowl set over a pan of barely simmering water. Stir over low heat until melted and smooth. Remove from the heat and set aside.

2 Meanwhile, pour the cream into a pan and bring to just below boiling point over low heat. Remove from the heat, then stir the cream and crème fraîche into the chocolate and cool slightly. Beat in the egg yolks, one at a time.

3 Pour the water into a small, heatproof bowl and sprinkle the gelatin on the surface. Let stand for 2–3 minutes to soften, then set over a pan of barely simmering water until completely dissolved. Stir the gelatin into the chocolate mixture and let stand until nearly set.

4 Brush the inside of 6 timbales, dariole molds, or small cups with oil, and line the bottoms with baking parchment. Whisk the egg whites until soft peaks form, then fold them into the chocolate mixture. Divide the mixture evenly among the prepared molds and smooth the surface. Cover with plastic wrap and chill in the refrigerator for 2 hours, until set.

5 Put the strawberries, raspberries, and black currants in a bowl and sprinkle with the superfine sugar. Pour in the liqueur and stir gently to mix. Cover with plastic wrap and let chill in the refrigerator for 2 hours.

6 To serve, run a round-bladed knife around the sides of the molds and carefully turn out onto individual serving plates. Divide the fruit among the plates and serve immediately, decorated with black currant leaves, if available.

chocolate sherbet

serves six

5 oz/140 g bittersweet chocolate,
   chopped coarsely
5 oz/140 g semisweet continental
   chocolate, chopped coarsely
scant 2 cups water
1 cup superfine sugar
langues de chat cookies,
   to serve

1 Put the bittersweet and semisweet chocolate into a food processor and process them briefly until they are very finely chopped.

2 Pour the water into a heavy-based pan and add the sugar. Stir over medium heat to dissolve, then bring to a boil. Boil for 2 minutes, without stirring, then remove the pan from the heat.

3 With the motor of the food processor running, pour the hot syrup onto the chocolate. Process for about 2 minutes, until all the chocolate has melted and the mixture is smooth. Scrape down the sides of the food processor if necessary. Carefully strain the chocolate mixture into a freezerproof container and let cool completely.

4 When the mixture is cool, place it in the freezer for about 1 hour, until slushy, but starting to become firm around the edges. Tip the mixture into the food processor and process until smooth. Return to the container and freeze the chocolate sherbet for at least 2 hours, until firm.

5 Remove the sherbet from the freezer about 10 minutes before serving and let stand at room temperature to let it soften slightly. Serve the chocolate in scoops and accompany with langues de chat cookies.

chocolate & honey ice cream

serves six

2 cups milk

7 oz/200 g semisweet chocolate, broken into pieces

4 eggs, separated

scant ½ cup superfine sugar

2 tbsp honey

pinch of salt

12 fresh strawberries, washed and hulled

1 Pour the milk into a pan, add 5½ oz/150 g of the chocolate, and stir over medium heat for 3–5 minutes, until melted. Remove the pan from the heat and set aside.

2 Beat the egg yolks with all but 1 tablespoon of the sugar in a separate bowl until pale and thickened. Gradually beat in the milk mixture, a little at a time. Return the mixture to a clean pan and cook over low heat, whisking constantly, until smooth and thickened. Remove from the heat and set aside to cool. Cover with plastic wrap and chill in the refrigerator for 30 minutes.

3 Whisk the egg whites with a pinch of salt until soft peaks form. Gradually whisk in the remaining sugar and continue whisking until stiff and glossy. Remove the chocolate mixture from the refrigerator and stir in the honey, then gently fold in the egg whites.

4 Divide the mixture among 6 individual freezerproof molds and place in the freezer for at least 4 hours, until frozen. Meanwhile, put the remaining chocolate into the top of a double boiler or in a heatproof bowl set over a pan of barely simmering water. Stir over low heat until melted and smooth, then dip the strawberries in the melted chocolate so that they are half-coated. Place on a sheet of baking parchment to set. Transfer the ice cream to the refrigerator for 10 minutes before serving. Turn out onto serving plates and decorate with the chocolate-coated strawberries.

marshmallow ice cream

serves four

3 oz/85 g semisweet chocolate, broken into pieces

6 oz/175 g white marshmallows

⅔ cup milk

1¼ cups heavy cream

1 Put the semisweet chocolate and marshmallows in a pan and pour in the milk. Warm over very low heat until the chocolate and marshmallows have melted. Remove from the heat and let cool completely.

2 Whisk the cream until thick, then fold it into the cold chocolate mixture with a metal spoon. Pour into a 1-lb/450-g loaf pan and freeze for at least 2 hours, until firm (it will keep for 1 month in the freezer). Serve the ice cream with fresh fruit.

chocolate & hazelnut parfait

serves six

1½ cups blanched hazelnuts

6 oz/175 g semisweet chocolate, broken into small pieces

2½ cups heavy cream

3 eggs, separated

2½ cups confectioners' sugar

1 tbsp unsweetened cocoa, for dusting

6 small fresh mint sprigs, to decorate

wafer cookies, to serve

1 Spread out the hazelnuts on a cookie sheet and toast under a broiler preheated to medium-hot, shaking the sheet from time to time, for about 5 minutes, until golden all over. Set aside to cool.

2 Put the chocolate into the top of a double boiler or in a heatproof bowl set over a pan of barely simmering water. Stir over low heat until melted, then remove the chocolate from the heat and cool. Put the toasted hazelnuts in a food processor and process until they are finely ground. Set aside while you whip the cream.

3 Whip the cream until it is stiff, then fold in the ground hazelnuts and set aside. Beat the egg yolks with 3 tablespoons of the sugar for 10 minutes until pale and thick.

4 Whisk the egg whites in a separate bowl until soft peaks form. Whisk in the remaining sugar, a little at a time, until the whites are stiff and glossy. Stir the cooled chocolate into the egg yolk mixture, then fold in the cream and, finally, fold in the egg whites. Divide the mixture among 6 freezerproof timbales or molds, cover with plastic wrap, and freeze for at least 8 hours or overnight until firm.

5 Transfer the parfaits to the refrigerator about 10 minutes before serving to soften slightly. Turn out onto individual serving plates, dust the tops lightly with cocoa, decorate with mint sprigs, and serve with wafer cookies.

mint-chocolate gelato

serves four

6 large eggs

¾ cup superfine sugar

1¼ cups milk

⅔ cup heavy cream

large handful of fresh mint leaves,
   rinsed and dried

2 drops green food coloring,
   optional

2 oz/55 g semisweet chocolate,
   chopped finely

1 Put the eggs and sugar into a heatproof bowl that will sit over a pan with plenty of room underneath. Using an electric mixer, beat the eggs and sugar together until they are thick and creamy.

2 Put the milk and cream in the pan and bring to a simmer, where small bubbles appear all around the edge, stirring. Pour onto the eggs, whisking constantly. Rinse the pan and put 1 inch/2.5 cm water in the bottom. Place the bowl on top, making sure the bottom does not touch the water. Turn the heat to medium–high.

3 Transfer the mixture to a pan and cook, stirring constantly with a wooden spoon, until the mixture is thick enough to coat the back of the spoon and leave a mark when you pull your finger across it.

4 Tear the mint leaves and stir them into the custard. Remove the custard from the heat. Let cool, then cover and set aside to infuse for at least 2 hours, chilling for the last 30 minutes.

5 Strain the mixture through a small nylon strainer to remove the pieces of mint. Stir in the food coloring (if using). Transfer to a freezerproof container and freeze the mixture for 1–2 hours, until frozen 1 inch/2.5 cm from the side of the container.

6 Scrape into a bowl and beat again until smooth. Stir in the chocolate pieces, smooth the top, and cover with plastic wrap or foil. Freeze until set, for up to 3 months. Soften the ice cream in the refrigerator for 20 minutes before serving.

chocolate rice dessert

serves eight

½ cup long-grain white rice

pinch of salt

2½ cups milk

½ cup granulated sugar

7 oz/200 g semisweet or
bittersweet chocolate, chopped

4 tbsp butter, diced

1 tsp vanilla extract

2 tbsp brandy

¾ cup heavy cream

whipped cream, for piping
(optional)

quick chocolate curls (see page 7),
to decorate (optional)

VARIATION

To mold the chocolate rice, soften 1 envelope powdered gelatin in about ¼ cup cold water and heat gently until dissolved. Stir into the chocolate just before folding in the cream. Pour into a rinsed mold, let set, then unmold.

---

1 Bring a pan of water to the boil. Sprinkle in the rice and add the salt. Reduce the heat and simmer gently for 15–20 minutes until the rice is just tender. Drain the rice, rinse, and drain again.

2 Heat the milk and sugar in a large heavy-based pan over medium heat until the sugar dissolves, stirring frequently. Add the chocolate and butter to the pan and stir until melted and smooth.

3 Stir in the cooked rice and reduce the heat to low. Cover and let simmer, stirring occasionally, for 30 minutes, until the milk is absorbed and the mixture thickened. Stir in the vanilla extract and brandy. Remove from the heat and let cool to room temperature.

4 Using an electric mixer, beat the cream until soft peaks form. Stir one heaped spoonful of the cream into the chocolate rice mixture to lighten it; then fold in the remaining cream.

5 Spoon into glass serving dishes, cover, and let chill for about 2 hours. If wished, decorate with piped whipped cream and top with quick chocolate curls. Serve cold.

zuccotto

serves eight

2½ cups heavy cream

¼ cup confectioners' sugar

½ cup hazelnuts, toasted

8 oz/225 g cherries, halved and
    pitted

4 oz/115 g semisweet chocolate,
    chopped finely

2 x 20-cm/8-inch round chocolate
    sponge cakes

4 tbsp brandy

4 tbsp Amaretto liqueur

TO DECORATE

2 tbsp confectioners' sugar

2 tbsp unsweetened cocoa

1 Whip the cream in a large bowl, until stiff, then fold in the confectioners' sugar, followed by the hazelnuts, cherries, and chocolate. Cover the cream mixture with plastic wrap and let chill in the refrigerator until required.

2 Meanwhile, cut the sponge cakes in half horizontally and then cut the pieces to fit a 5-cup bowl, so that the bottom and sides are completely lined. Set aside the remaining sponge cake. Mix the brandy and Amaretto together in a small bowl and sprinkle the mixture evenly over the sponge cake lining so it can soak in.

3 Remove the cream filling from the refrigerator and spoon it into the lined bowl. Cover the top with the remaining sponge cake, cut to fit. Cover with plastic wrap and chill the bombe in the refrigerator for 2 hours, or until ready to serve.

4 Sift the confectioners' sugar into a bowl and the cocoa into another bowl. Remove the bombe from the refrigerator and run a round-bladed knife around the sides to loosen it. Place a serving plate on top of the bowl and invert. Dust alternate quarters with confectioners' sugar and cocoa powder.

zuccherini

6 oz/175 g semisweet chocolate,
   broken into pieces

10 amaretti cookies, crushed

MOUSSE

2 oz/55 g semisweet chocolate,
   broken into pieces

1 tbsp cold, strong black coffee

2 eggs, separated

2 tsp orange-flavored liqueur

TO DECORATE

⅔ cup heavy cream

2 tbsp unsweetened cocoa

6 chocolate-coated coffee beans

1 To make the chocolate cups to hold the filling, put the 6-oz/ 175-g semisweet chocolate into the top of a double boiler or in a heatproof bowl set over a pan of barely simmering water. Stir until melted and smooth, but not too runny, then remove the chocolate from the heat. Carefully coat the inside of 12 double paper cake cases with melted chocolate, using a small brush. Stand the chocolate cups on a plate and let chill for at least 8 hours or overnight in the refrigerator.

2 To make the mousse, put the chocolate and coffee in the top of a double boiler or in a heatproof bowl set over a pan of barely simmering water. Stir over low heat until the chocolate has melted and the mixture is smooth, then remove from the heat. Let cool slightly, then stir in the egg yolks and orange-flavored liqueur.

3 Whisk the egg whites in a separate bowl until stiff peaks form. Fold the whites into the chocolate mixture with a metal spoon, then set aside to cool.

4 Remove the chocolate cups from the refrigerator and carefully peel off the paper cases. Divide the crushed amaretti cookies equally among the

chocolate cups and top with the chocolate mousse. Return to the refrigerator for at least 30 minutes. Just before serving, whip the cream and pipe a star on the top of each chocolate cup. Dust half of the zuccherini with cocoa and decorate the other half with the chocolate-coated coffee beans.

phyllo nests

serves four

1 tbsp unsalted butter

6 sheets phyllo pastry, about
    12 x 6 inches/30 x 15 cm each

1½ oz/40 g semisweet chocolate,
    broken into pieces

½ cup ricotta cheese

16 seedless green grapes, halved

24 seedless black grapes, halved

1 Put the butter into a small pan and set over low heat until melted. Remove from the heat. Preheat the oven to 375°F/190°C. Cut each sheet of phyllo pastry into 4 pieces, to give 24 rectangles, each measuring about 6 x 3 inches/15 x 7.5 cm, then stack them all on top of each other. Brush 4 shallow muffin pans with melted butter. Line 1 pan with a rectangle of phyllo pastry, brush with melted butter, and place another rectangle on top at an angle to the first, and brush it with melted butter. Continue in this way, lining each pan with 6 rectangles, each brushed with melted butter. Brush the top layers of the pastry nests with melted butter.

2 Bake in preheated oven for 7–8 minutes, until golden and crisp. Remove the pastry nests from the oven and set aside to cool in the pans.

3 Put the chocolate into the top of a double boiler or in a heatproof bowl set over a pan of barely simmering water. Stir over low heat until melted. Remove from the heat and let cool slightly. Brush the insides of the pastry shells with about half the melted chocolate. Beat the ricotta cheese until smooth, then beat in the remaining melted chocolate.

4 Divide the chocolate ricotta mixture among the pastry shells and arrange the grapes alternately around the edges. Carefully lift the filled pastry nests out of the pans and serve immediately.

chocolate & pernod creams

serves four

2 oz/55 g semisweet chocolate,
  broken into pieces

scant 1 cup milk

1¼ cup heavy cream

2 tbsp superfine sugar

1 tbsp arrowroot dissolved in 2 tbsp
  milk

3 tbsp Pernod

langues de chat cookies, or
  chocolate-tipped rolled wafers,
  to serve

1 Put the chocolate into the top of a double boiler or in a heatproof bowl set over a pan of barely simmering water. Stir over low heat until melted. Remove the pan from the heat and let cool slightly.

2 Pour the milk and cream into a pan over low heat and bring to just below boiling point, stirring occasionally. Remove the pan from the heat and then set aside.

3 Beat the sugar and the arrowroot mixture into the melted chocolate. Gradually stir in the hot milk and cream mixture, then stir in the Pernod. Return the double boiler to the heat or set the bowl over a pan of barely simmering water and cook, over low heat, for 10 minutes, stirring constantly, until thick and smooth. Remove from the heat and let cool.

4 Pour the chocolate and Pernod mixture into 4 individual serving glasses. Cover the glasses with plastic wrap and let chill for 2 hours. Serve the chocolate and Pernod creams with langues de chats cookies or chocolate-tipped rolled wafers.

small cakes & cookies

This chapter contains everyday delights for chocolate fans. You are sure to be tempted by our wonderful array of cookies and small cakes. Make any day special with a home-made chocolate cookie to be served with coffee, as a snack or to accompany a special dessert. Although some take a little longer to make, most are quick and easy to prepare and decoration is often simple—although you can get carried away if you like!

You'll find recipes for old favorites, such as Chocolate Chip Muffins and Chocolate Chip Cookies, Chocolate Butterfly Cakes, and Chocolate Brownies. There are also new recipes for cookies and small cakes, such as Chocolate Coconut Squares or Malted Chocolate Wedges. Finally, we have given the chocolate treatment to some traditional recipes—try Chocolate Biscuits or Chocolate Chip Flapjacks.

chocolate rum babas

serves four

¾ cup strong all-purpose flour

¼ cup unsweetened cocoa

1 envelope active dry yeast

pinch of salt

1 tbsp superfine sugar

1½ oz/40 g semisweet chocolate

2 eggs

3 tbsp lukewarm milk

4 tbsp butter, melted

SYRUP

4 tbsp honey

2 tbsp water

4 tbsp rum

TO SERVE

whipped cream

unsweetened cocoa, for dusting

fresh fruit, optional

1 Lightly oil 4 individual ring pans. Sift the flour and cocoa together in a large warmed mixing bowl. Grate the chocolate and stir into the mix. Beat the eggs together in a separate bowl, add the milk and butter, and continue beating until mixed.

2 Make a well in the center of the dry ingredients and pour in the egg mixture, beating to mix to a batter. Beat for 10 minutes, ideally in a electric mixer with a dough hook. Divide the mixture between the pans—it should come halfway up the sides.

3 Place on a cookie sheet and cover with a damp dish towel. Let stand in a warm place until the mixture rises almost to the tops of the pans. Bake the rum babas in a preheated oven, 400°F/200°C, for 15 minutes.

4 To make the syrup, gently heat all of the ingredients in a small pan. Turn out the babas and place on rack placed above a tray to catch the syrup. Drizzle the syrup over the babas and let stand for at least 2 hours for the syrup to soak in. Once or twice, spoon the syrup that has dripped onto the tray over the babas.

5 Fill the center of the babas with whipped cream and sprinkle a little cocoa over the top. Serve the babas with fresh fruit, if wished.

174

chocolate fudge brownies

makes sixteen

7 oz/200 g lowfat soft cheese

½ tsp vanilla extract

generous 1 cup superfine sugar

2 eggs

generous ⅓ cup butter

3 tbsp unsweetened cocoa

¾ cup self-rising flour, sifted

⅓ cup chopped pecans

FUDGE FROSTING

4 tbsp butter

1 tbsp milk

⅔ cup icing confectioners' sugar

2 tbsp unsweetened cocoa

pecans, to decorate (optional)

1 Lightly grease an 8-inch/20-cm square shallow cake pan and line the bottom.

2 Beat the cheese, vanilla extract, and 5 teaspoons of superfine sugar together, then set aside.

3 Beat the eggs and remaining superfine sugar together until light and fluffy. Place the butter and cocoa in a small pan and heat gently, stirring until the butter melts and the mixture combines, then stir it into the egg mixture. Fold in the flour and nuts.

4 Pour half of the brownie mixture into the pan and smooth the top. Carefully spread the soft cheese over it, then cover it with the remaining brownie mixture. Bake in a preheated oven, 350°F/180°C, for 40–45 minutes. Cool in the pan.

5 To make the frosting, melt the butter in the milk. Stir in the confectioners' sugar and cocoa. Using a spatula spread the frosting over the brownies and decorate with pecans (if using). Let the frosting set, then cut into squares to serve.

VARIATION

Omit the cheese layer if preferred. Use walnuts in place of the pecans.

pain au chocolat

makes twelve

4 cups strong all-purpose flour

½ tsp salt

1 envelope active dry yeast

2 tbsp shortening

1 egg, beaten lightly

1 cup lukewarm water

¾ cup butter, softened

beaten egg, for glazing

3½ oz/100 g semisweet chocolate,
  broken into 12 squares

confectioners' sugar, for dusting

1 Lightly grease a cookie sheet with a little butter and set aside. Sift the flour and salt into a mixing bowl and stir in the yeast. Rub the shortening into the flour and yeast mixture with your fingertips. Add the egg and enough of the water to mix to

a soft dough. Knead for about 10 minutes to make a smooth, elastic dough.

2 Roll out to form a 15 x 8-inch/ 38 x 20-cm rectangle. Divide the butter into 3 portions and dot one portion over two-thirds of the rectangle, leaving a small border around the edge.

3 Fold the rectangle into 3 by first folding the plain part of the dough over and then the other side. Seal the edges of the dough by pressing with a rolling pin. Give the dough a quarter turn so the sealed edges are at the top and bottom. Re-roll and fold (without adding butter), then wrap the dough and let chill in for 30 minutes.

4 Repeat steps 2 and 3 until all of the butter has been used, chilling the dough each time. Re-roll and fold twice more without butter. Let chill for a final 30 minutes.

5 Roll the dough to a 18 x 12-inch/46 x 30-cm rectangle, then trim and halve, lengthwise. Cut each half into 6 rectangles and brush with beaten egg. Place a chocolate square at one end of each rectangle and roll up to form a sausage. Press the ends together and place, seam-side down, on the cookie sheet. Cover the pain au chocolat and let rise for 40 minutes in a warm place. Brush with egg and bake in a preheated oven, 425°F/220°C, for 20–25, minutes until golden. Cool on a wire rack. Serve the pain au chocolat warm or cold.

chocolate dairy wraps

serves six

2 eggs

4 tbsp superfine sugar

⅓ cup all-purpose flour

1½ tbsp unsweetened cocoa

4 tbsp apricot jelly

⅔ cup heavy cream, whipped

confectioners' sugar, for dusting

1 Line 2 cookie sheets with pieces of baking parchment. Whisk the eggs and sugar together until the mixture is very light and fluffy and the whisk leaves a trail when lifted.

2 Sift the flour and cocoa together. Using a metal spoon or a spatula, gently fold it into the eggs and sugar in a figure-eight movement.

3 Drop rounded tablespoonfuls of the mixture onto the lined cookie sheets and spread them into oval shapes. Make sure they are well spaced apart as they will spread out during cooking.

4 Bake in a preheated oven, 425°F/220°C, for 6–8 minutes or until springy to the touch. Let cool on the cookie sheets.

5 When cold, slide the cakes onto a damp dish towel and let stand until cold. Carefully remove them from the dampened parchment. Spread the flat side of the cakes with apricot jelly, then spoon or pipe the whipped cream down the center of each one.

6 Fold the chocolate dairy wraps in half and place them on a serving plate. Sprinkle with confectioners' sugar and serve.

no-bake chocolate squares

makes sixteen

9½ oz/275 g semisweet chocolate

¾ cup butter

4 tbsp light corn syrup

2 tbsp dark rum, optional

6 oz/175 g plain cookies

1 oz/25 g toasted rice cereal

½ cup chopped walnuts or pecans

½ cup candied cherries, chopped
  coarsely

1 oz/25 g white chocolate, to
  decorate

2 Break the cookies into small pieces and stir into the chocolate mixture along with the toasted rice cereal, nuts, and cherries.

3 Line a 7-inch/18-cm square cake pan with baking parchment. Pour the mixture into the pan and smooth the top, pressing down well with the back of a spoon. Let chill for 2 hours.

4 To decorate, melt the white chocolate and drizzle it over the top of the cake randomly. Let it set. To serve, carefully turn out of the pan and remove the baking parchment. Cut the cake into 16 squares.

VARIATION

Brandy or an orange-flavored liqueur can be used instead of the rum, if you prefer. Cherry brandy also works well.

1 Place the semisweet chocolate in a large mixing bowl with the butter, syrup, and rum (if using), and set over a pan of gently simmering water until melted, stirring until blended.

chocolate butterfly cakes

makes twelve

½ cup soft margarine

½ cup superfine sugar

1¼ cups self-rising flour

2 large eggs

2 tbsp unsweetened cocoa

1 oz/25 g semisweet chocolate,
    melted

LEMON BUTTER CREAM

⅓ cup unsalted butter, softened

1⅓ cups confectioners' sugar, sifted

grated rind of ½ lemon

1 tbsp lemon juice

confectioners' sugar, for dusting

1 Place 12 individual paper cases in a shallow muffin pan. Place all of the ingredients for the cakes, except for the melted chocolate, in a large mixing bowl, and beat with an electric mixer until the mixture is just smooth. Beat in the melted chocolate, stirring until well blended.

2 Spoon equal amounts of the mixture into each paper case, filling them three-quarters full. Bake in a preheated oven, 350°F/180°C, for 15 minutes or until springy to the touch. Transfer the chocolate cakes to a wire rack and let them cool completely.

3 Meanwhile, make the lemon butter cream. Place the butter in a mixing bowl and beat until fluffy, then gradually beat in the confectioners' sugar. Beat in the lemon rind and gradually add the lemon juice, beating well.

4 When cold, cut the top off each cake using a serrated knife. Cut each cake top in half.

5 Spread or pipe the butter cream over the cut surface of each cake and push the 2 cut pieces of cake top into the frosting to form wings. Sprinkle with confectioners' sugar.

chocolate biscuits

serves four

2 cups self-rising flour, sifted

5 tbsp butter

1 tbsp superfine sugar

⅓ cup chocolate chips

about ⅔ cup milk

COOK'S TIP

To be at their best, all biscuits should be freshly baked and served warm. Split the biscuits and spread them with chocolate hazelnut spread.

1 Grease a cookie sheet. Place the flour in a mixing bowl. Cut the butter into small pieces and rub it into the flour with your fingertips until the mixture resembles fine bread crumbs.

2 Stir in the superfine sugar and chocolate chips.

3 Mix in enough of the milk to form a soft dough.

4 On a lightly floured counter, roll out the dough to form a 4 x 6-inch/10 x 15-cm rectangle, about 1-inch/2.5-cm thick. Cut the dough into 9 squares.

5 Place the biscuits, spaced well apart, on the prepared cookie sheet.

6 Brush with a little milk and bake in a preheated oven, 425°F/ 220°C, for 10–12 minutes, until risen and golden. Serve warm.

chocolate crispy bites

makes sixteen

WHITE CHOCOLATE LAYER

4 tbsp butter

1 tbsp light corn syrup

5½ oz/150 g white chocolate

1¾ oz/50 g toasted rice cereal

SEMISWEET CHOCOLATE LAYER

4 tbsp butter

2 tbsp light corn syrup

4½ oz/125 g semisweet chocolate,
    broken into small pieces

2¾ oz/75 g toasted rice cereal

COOK'S TIP

These bites can be made
up to 4 days ahead. Keep them
covered in the refrigerator
until ready to use.

1 Grease an 8-inch/20-cm square cake pan with butter and line with baking parchment.

2 To make the white chocolate layer, melt the butter, light corn syrup, and white chocolate in a bowl set over a pan of simmering water.

3 Remove from the heat and stir in the toasted rice cereal until it is well combined.

4 Press into the prepared pan and smooth the surface.

5 To make the semisweet chocolate layer, melt the butter, light corn syrup, and chocolate in a bowl set over a pan of simmering water.

6 Remove from the heat and stir in the rice cereal. Pour the semisweet chocolate over the hardened white chocolate layer, cool, and chill until hardened.

7 Turn the mixture out of the cake pan and cut into small squares using a sharp knife.

chocolate coconut squares

makes nine

8 oz/225 g semisweet chocolate
   graham crackers

⅓ cup butter or margarine

¾ cup canned evaporated milk

1 egg, beaten

1 tsp vanilla extract

2 tbsp superfine sugar

⅓ cup self-rising flour, sifted

1⅓ cups shredded coconut

1¾ oz/50 g semisweet chocolate,
   optional

1 Grease a shallow 8-inch/20-cm square cake pan and line.

2 Crush the crackers in a plastic bag with a rolling pin or process them in a food processor.

3 Melt the butter or margarine in a pan and stir in the crushed crackers until well combined.

4 Press the mixture into the bottom of the cake pan.

5 Beat the evaporated milk, egg, vanilla, and sugar together until smooth. Stir in the flour and shredded coconut. Pour over the cracker layer and use a spatula to smooth the top.

6 Bake the coconut mixture in a preheated oven, 375°F/190°C, for 30 minutes or until the coconut topping has become firm and just golden.

7 Let cool in the cake pan for about 5 minutes, then cut into squares. Let cool completely in the pan.

8 Carefully remove the squares from the pan and place them on a board. Melt the semisweet chocolate (if using) and drizzle it over the squares to decorate them. Let the chocolate set before serving.

VARIATION

Store the squares in an airtight container for up to 4 days. They can be frozen, undecorated, for up to 2 months. Thaw at room temperature.

chocolate éclairs

makes ten

DOUGH

⅔ cup water

5 tbsp butter, cut into small pieces

¾ cup strong all-purpose flour, sifted

2 eggs

CRÈME PÂTISSIÈRE

2 eggs, beaten lightly

¼ cup superfine sugar

2 tbsp cornstarch

1¼ cups milk

¼ tsp vanilla extract

FROSTING

2 tbsp butter

1 tbsp milk

1 tbsp unsweetened cocoa

½ cup confectioners' sugar

a little white chocolate, melted

1 Lightly grease a cookie sheet. Place the water in a pan, add the butter, and heat gently until the butter melts. Bring to a rolling boil, then remove the pan from the heat and add the flour in one go, beating well until the mixture leaves the sides of the pan and forms a ball. Let cool slightly, then gradually beat in the eggs to form a smooth, glossy mixture. Spoon into a large pastry bag fitted with a ½-inch/1-cm plain tip.

2 Sprinkle the cookie sheet with a little water. Pipe éclairs 3-inches/7.5-cm long, spaced well apart. Bake in a preheated oven, 400°F/200°C, for 30–35 minutes or until crisp and golden. Make a small slit in each one to let the steam escape. Cool on a wire rack.

3 Meanwhile, make the crème pâtissière. Whisk the eggs and sugar until thick and creamy, then fold in the cornstarch. Heat the milk until almost boiling and pour onto the eggs, whisking. Transfer to the pan and cook over low heat, stirring until thick. Remove the pan from the heat and stir in the vanilla extract. Cover with baking parchment and let cool.

4 To make the frosting, melt the butter with the milk in a pan, remove from the heat, and stir in the cocoa and sugar. Split the éclairs lengthwise and pipe in the crème pâtissière. Spread the frosting over the top of the éclair. Spoon over the white chocolate, swirl in, and let set. If preferred, the éclairs can be filled with plain or sweetened whipped cream.

chocolate chip muffins

makes twelve

generous ⅓ cup soft margarine

1 cup superfine sugar

2 large eggs

⅔ cup whole-milk plain yogurt

5 tbsp milk

2 cups all-purpose flour

1 tsp baking soda

1 cup semisweet chocolate chips

1 Line a 12-muffin pan with paper cases.

2 Place the margarine and sugar in a mixing bowl and beat with a wooden spoon until light and fluffy. Beat in the eggs, yogurt, and milk until well combined.

3 Sift the flour and baking soda together and add to the mixture. Stir until just blended.

4 Stir in the chocolate chips, then spoon the mixture into the paper cases and bake in a preheated oven, 375°F/190°C, for 25 minutes or until a fine skewer inserted into the center comes out clean. Let the muffins cool in the pan for 5 minutes, then turn them out onto a wire rack to cool completely.

VARIATION

The mixture can also be used to make 6 large or 24 mini muffins. Bake mini muffins for 10 minutes or until springy to the touch.

chocolate biscotti

makes sixteen

1 egg

⅓ cup superfine sugar

1 tsp vanilla extract

1 cup all-purpose flour

½ tsp baking powder

1 tsp ground cinnamon

1¾ oz/50 g semisweet chocolate,
   chopped coarsely

½ cup toasted slivered almonds

⅓ cup pine nuts

1 Lightly grease a large cookie sheet. Set aside while you prepare the cookie mixture.

2 Whisk the egg, sugar, and vanilla extract in a mixing bowl with an electric mixer until thick and pale—ribbons of mixture should trail from the whisk as you lift it.

3 Sift the flour, baking powder, and cinnamon into a separate bowl, then sift into the egg mixture and fold in gently. Stir in the coarsely chopped semisweet chocolate, toasted slivered almonds, and pine nuts.

4 Turn out on to a lightly floured counter and shape into a flat log, 9-inches/23-cm long and ¾-inch/1.5-cm wide. Transfer to the cookie sheet.

5 Bake in a preheated oven, 350°F/180°C, for 20–25 minutes or until golden. Remove the cookie log from the oven and let cool for 5 minutes or until firm.

6 Transfer the log to a cutting board. Using a serrated bread knife, cut the log on the diagonal into slices about ½-inch/1-cm thick and arrange them on the cookie sheet. Cook for 10–15 minutes, turning halfway through the cooking time.

7 Let cool for about 5 minutes, then transfer to a wire rack to cool.

chocolate chip tartlets

serves six

1¾ oz/50 g toasted hazelnuts

1¼ cups all-purpose flour

1 tbsp confectioners' sugar

⅓ cup soft margarine

FILLING

2 tbsp cornstarch

1 tbsp unsweetened cocoa

1 tbsp superfine sugar

1¼ cups semi-skim milk

3 tbsp chocolate and hazelnut
  spread

2½ tbsp semisweet chocolate chips

2½ tbsp milk chocolate chips

2½ tbsp white chocolate chips

1 Finely chop the nuts in a food
processor. Add the flour, the
1 tablespoon of confectioners' sugar,
and margarine. Process for a few
seconds until the mixture resembles
bread crumbs. Add 2–3 tablespoons
of water and process to form a soft
dough. Cover and let chill in the freezer
for 10 minutes.

2 Roll out the dough and use to line
six 4-inch/10-cm loose-bottomed
tartlet pans. Prick the bottom of the
tartlet shells with a fork and line them
with loosely crumpled foil. Bake in a
preheated oven, 400°F/200°C, for 15
minutes. Remove the foil and bake for
another 5 minutes, until the tartlet
shells are crisp and golden. Remove
from the oven and let cool.

3 Make the filling. Mix the
cornstarch, cocoa, and sugar
together with enough milk to make a
smooth paste. Stir in the remaining
milk. Pour into a pan and cook gently
over low heat, stirring until thickened.
Stir in the chocolate hazelnut spread.

4 Mix the chocolate chips together
and set aside one-quarter. Stir half
of the remaining chips into the custard.
Cover with damp waxed paper, let stand
until almost cold, then stir in the second
half of the chocolate chips. Spoon the
mixture into the tartlet shells and let
cool. Decorate with the reserved chips,
spinkling them over the top.

chocolate orange cookies

makes thirty

⅓ cup butter, softened

⅓ cup superfine sugar

1 egg

1 tbsp milk

2 cups all-purpose flour

¼ cup unsweetened cocoa

FROSTING

1 cup confectioners' sugar, sifted

3 tbsp orange juice

a little semisweet chocolate, melted

1 Line 2 cookie sheets with baking parchment.

2 Beat the butter and sugar together until light and fluffy. Beat in the egg and milk until well combined. Sift the flour and cocoa into the mixture and gradually mix to form a soft dough. Use your fingers to incorporate the last of the flour and bring the dough together.

3 Roll out the dough on a lightly floured counter until ¼-inch/5-mm thick. Using a 2-inch/5-cm fluted round cutter, cut out as many cookies as you can. Re-roll the dough trimmings and cut out more cookies.

4 Place the cookies on the prepared cookie sheet and bake in a preheated oven, 350°F/180°C, for 10–12 minutes or until golden.

5 Let the cookies cool on the cookie sheet for a few minutes, then transfer them to a wire rack and let cool completely.

6 For the frosting, place the confectioners' sugar in a bowl and stir in enough orange juice to form a thin frosting that will coat the back of a spoon. Spread the frosting over the cookies and allow to set. Drizzle with melted chocolate. Let the chocolate set before serving.

chocolate caramel squares

makes sixteen

generous ⅓ cup soft margarine

⅓ cup light brown sugar

1 cup all-purpose flour

½ cup rolled oats

CARAMEL FILLING

2 tbsp butter

2 tbsp brown sugar

generous ¾ cup condensed milk

TOPPING

3½ oz/100 g semisweet chocolate

1 oz/25 g white chocolate, optional

1 Beat the margarine and brown sugar together in a bowl until light and fluffy. Beat in the flour and the rolled oats. Use your fingertips to bring the mixture together if necessary.

2 Press the oat mixture into the bottom of a shallow 8-inch/20-cm square cake pan.

3 Bake in a preheated oven, 350°F/180°C, for 25 minutes or until just golden and firm. Cool the mixture in the pan.

4 Place the ingredients for the caramel filling in a pan and heat gently, stirring until the sugar has dissolved and the ingredients combine. Bring slowly to a boil over very low heat, then boil very gently for 3–4 minutes, stirring constantly, until the filling has thickened.

5 Pour the caramel filling over the oat layer in the pan, smooth with a spatula, and let set.

6 Melt the semisweet chocolate and spread it over the caramel. If using the white chocolate, melt it and pipe lines of white chocolate over the semisweet chocolate. Using a toothpick, feather the white chocolate into the semisweet chocolate. Let set. Cut into squares.

COOK'S TIP

If liked, you can line the pan with baking parchment so that the oat layer can be lifted out before cutting into pieces.

malted chocolate wedges

makes sixteen

generous ⅓ cup butter

2 tbsp light corn syrup

2 tbsp malted chocolate drink

8 oz/225 g malted milk cookies

2¾ oz/75 g light or semisweet
    chocolate, broken into pieces

2 tbsp confectioners' sugar

2 tbsp milk

1 Grease a shallow 7-inch/18-cm round cake pan or tart pan and line the bottom with baking parchment.

2 Place the butter, light corn syrup, and malted chocolate drink in a small pan and heat gently, stirring all the time until the butter has melted and the mixture is well combined.

3 Crush the cookies in a plastic bag with a rolling pin, or process them in a food processor. Stir the cookie crumbs into the chocolate mixture and mix well.

4 Press the mixture into the prepared pan and then chill in the refrigerator until firm.

5 Place the chocolate pieces in a small heatproof bowl with the confectioners' sugar and the milk. Place the bowl over a pan of gently simmering water and stir gently until the chocolate melts and the mixture is thoroughly combined.

6 Spread the chocolate frosting over the cookie bottom and let set in the pan. Using a sharp knife, carefully cut the mixture into wedges to serve.

VARIATION

Add chopped pecans to
the cookie crumb mixture in
Step 3, if liked.

checkerboard cookies

makes eighteen

¾ cup butter, softened

6 tbsp confectioners' sugar

1 teaspoon vanilla extract or grated
     rind of ½ orange

2¼ cups all-purpose flour

1 oz/25 g semisweet chocolate

a little beaten egg white

1 Lightly grease a cookie sheet.
Beat the butter and confectioners'
sugar in a mixing bowl until light and
fluffy. Beat in the vanilla extract or
grated orange rind.

2 Gradually beat in the flour to
form a soft dough. Use your
fingers to incorporate the last of the
flour and bring the dough together.

3 Melt the chocolate. Divide the
dough in half and beat the melted
chocolate into one half. Keeping each
half of the dough separate, cover, and
let chill for 30 minutes.

4 Roll out each piece of dough to a
rectangle measuring 3 x 8 inches/
7.5 x 20 cm and 3-cm/1½-inches thick.
Brush one piece of dough with a little
egg white and place the other on top.

5 Cut the block of dough in half
lengthwise and turn over one
half. Brush the side of one strip with
egg white and butt the other up to it,
so that it resembles a checkerboard.

6 Cut the block into thin slices and
place each slice flat on the
prepared cookie sheet, allowing
enough room for the slices to spread
out a little during cooking.

7 Bake in a preheated oven, 350°F/
180°C, for about 10 minutes,
until just firm. Let cool on the cookie
sheets for a few minutes, before
carefully transferring to a wire rack
with a spatula. Let cool completely.

chocolate meringues

makes eight

4 egg whites

1 cup superfine sugar

1 tsp cornstarch

1½ oz/40 g semisweet chocolate

TO FINISH

3½ oz/100 g semisweet chocolate

⅔ cup heavy cream

1 tbsp confectioners' sugar

1 tbsp brandy, optional

1 Line 2 cookie sheets with baking parchment. Whisk the egg whites until standing in soft peaks, then gradually whisk in half of the sugar. Continue whisking until the mixture is very stiff and glossy.

2 Carefully fold in the remaining sugar and cornstarch. Grate the chocolate.

3 Spoon the mixture into a pastry bag fitted with a large star or plain tip. Pipe 16 large rosettes or mounds on the lined cookie sheets.

4 Bake in a preheated oven, 275°F/140°C, for about 1 hour, changing the position of the cookie sheets halfway through cooking. Without opening the oven door, turn off the oven and let the meringues cool in the oven. Once the meringues are cold, carefully peel away the baking parchment.

5 Melt the semisweet chocolate and spread it over the bottom of the meringues. Stand them upside down on a wire rack until the chocolate has set. Whip the cream, confectioners'

sugar, and brandy (if using) until the cream holds its shape. Spoon into a pastry bag and use to sandwich the meringues together in pairs. Serve.

VARIATION

To make mini meringues, use a star-shaped tip and pipe about 24 small rosettes. Bake for about 40 minutes until crisp.

mexican chocolate meringues

makes twenty five

4–5 egg whites, at room
temperature

a pinch of salt

¼ tsp cream of tartar

¼–½ tsp vanilla extract

¾–1 cup superfine sugar

⅛–¼ tsp ground cinnamon

4 oz/115 g semisweet or
bittersweet chocolate, grated

TO SERVE

ground cinnamon, for dusting

4 oz/115 g strawberries or other
fruit

chocolate-flavored cream (see
Cook's Tip)

1 Whisk the egg whites until they are foamy, then add the salt and cream of tartar and beat until very stiff. Whisk in the vanilla extract, then slowly whisk in the sugar, a small amount at a time, until the meringue is shiny and stiff. This should take about 3 minutes by hand, and under a minute if you have an electric mixer.

2 Whisk in the cinnamon and grated chocolate. Spoon mounds of about 2 tablespoons, onto an ungreased, non-stick cookie sheet. Space the mounds well apart.

3 Place in a preheated oven, 300°F/ 150°C, and cook for 2 hours.

4 Carefully remove from the cookie sheet. If the meringues are too moist and soft, return them to the oven to firm up and dry out more. Let them cool completely.

COOK'S TIP

To make the flavored cream, simply stir half-melted chocolate pieces into stiffly whipped cream, then chill until solid.

5 Serve the chocolate meringues dusted with cinnamon and accompanied by strawberries or other soft fruit of your choice and a little of the chocolate-flavored cream.

201

viennese chocolate fingers

makes eighteen

½ cup unsalted butter

6 tbsp confectioners' sugar

1½ cups self-rising flour, sifted

3 tbsp cornstarch

7 oz/200 g semisweet chocolate

1 Lightly grease 2 cookie sheets. Beat the butter and sugar in a mixing bowl until light and fluffy. Gradually beat in the flour and cornstarch.

2 Melt 2¾ oz/75 g of the semisweet chocolate and beat into the cookie dough.

3 Place in a pastry bag fitted with a large star tip and pipe fingers about 2-inches/5-cm long on the cookie sheets, spaced apart to allow for spreading.

4 Bake in a preheated oven, 375°F/ 190°C, for 12–15 minutes. Let cool slightly, then transfer to a wire rack and cool completely.

COOK'S TIP

If the cookie dough is too thick to pipe, beat in a little milk to thin it out before you place it in the pastry bag.

5 Melt the remaining chocolate and dip one end of each cookie in the chocolate, allowing the excess to drip back into the bowl.

6 Place the cookies on a sheet of baking parchment and let the chocolate set before serving.

chocolate hazelnut palmiers

makes twenty-six

TOPPING

13 oz/375 g ready-made puff pie
  dough

8 tbsp chocolate hazelnut spread

½ cup chopped toasted hazelnuts

2 tbsp superfine sugar

1 Lightly grease a cookie sheet. Roll out the puff pie dough on a lightly floured counter to a rectangle about 15 x 9 inches/38 x 23 cm in size.

2 Spread the chocolate hazelnut spread over the pie dough using a spatula, then sprinkle the chopped hazelnuts over the top.

3 Roll up one long side of the pie dough to the center, then roll up the other side so that they meet in the center. Where the pieces meet, dampen the edges with a little water to join them. Using a sharp knife, cut into thin slices. Place each slice onto the prepared cookie sheet and flatten slightly with a spatula. Sprinkle the slices with the superfine sugar.

VARIATION

For an extra chocolate flavor, dip the palmiers in melted semisweet chocolate to half-cover each one. Place the chocolate-dipped palmiers onto a sheet of baking parchment and let set.

4 Bake in a preheated oven, 425°F/220°C, for 10–15 minutes, until golden. Transfer to a wire rack to cool.

rice pudding tartlets

serves six

1 package frozen unsweetened pie
dough

4 cups milk

pinch of salt

1 vanilla bean, split, seeds removed
and set aside

½ cup risotto or short-grain white
rice

1 tbsp cornstarch

2 tbsp sugar

unsweetened cocoa, for dusting

melted chocolate, to decorate

GANACHE

generous ¾ cup heavy cream

1 tbsp light corn syrup

6 oz/175 g semisweet or
bittersweet chocolate, chopped

1 tbsp unsalted butter

1 Thaw the pie dough, and then use it to line six 4-in /10-cm tart pans. Fill them with baking beans and bake blind in an oven preheated to 400°F/200°C for about 20 minutes, until the pie crust is set and golden at the edges. Transfer to a wire rack to cool.

2 To make the ganache, bring the heavy cream and corn syrup to a boil. Remove from the heat and immediately stir in the chopped chocolate. Continue stirring until melted and smooth, then beat in the butter until well combined. Spoon a 1-inch/2.5-cm thick layer into each tartlet. Set aside.

3 Bring the milk and salt to a boil in a pan. Sprinkle in the rice and return to a boil. Add the vanilla bean and seeds. Reduce the heat and let simmer gently until the rice is tender and the milk creamy.

4 Blend the cornstarch and sugar in a small bowl and add about 2 tablespoons of water to make a paste. Stir in a few spoonfuls of the rice mixture, then stir the cornstarch mixture into the rice. Bring to a boil and cook for about 1 minute, until thickened. Cool the pan in ice water, stirring until thick.

5 Spoon the rice mixture into the tartlets, filling each to the brim. Let set at room temperature. To serve the rice pudding tartlets, dust with cocoa and pipe or drizzle a little melted chocolate over each.

chocolate brownies

makes twelve

2 oz/55 g unsweetened pitted
   dates, chopped

2 oz/55 g no-soak prunes, chopped

6 tbsp unsweetened apple juice

4 medium eggs, beaten

2 cups brown sugar

1 tsp vanilla extract

4 tbsp lowfat drinking chocolate
   powder, plus extra for dusting

2 tbsp unsweetened cocoa

1½ cups all-purpose flour

⅓ cup semisweet chocolate chips

FROSTING

¾ cup confectioners' sugar

1–2 tsp water

1 tsp vanilla extract

COOK'S TIP

Make double the amount,
cut one of the cakes into bars,
and open-freeze, then store in
plastic bags. Take out pieces of
cake as and when you need
them—they'll take no time
at all to thaw.

1 Preheat the oven to 350°F/180°C. Grease and line a 7 x 11-inch/ 18 x 28-cm cake pan with baking parchment. Place the dates and prunes in a small pan and add the apple juice. Bring to a boil, cover, and let simmer for 10 minutes until soft. Beat to form a smooth paste, then set aside to cool.

2 Place the cooled fruit in a mixing bowl and stir in the eggs, sugar, and vanilla extract. Sift in 4 tablespoons of drinking chocolate, the cocoa, and flour, and fold in along with the semisweet chocolate chips until everything is well combined.

3 Spoon the mixture into the pan and smooth over the top. Bake in the preheated oven, for 25–30 minutes, until firm to the touch or until a skewer inserted into the center comes out clean. Cut into 12 bars and let cool in the pan for 10 minutes. Transfer to a wire rack to cool completely.

4 To make the frosting, sift the sugar into a bowl and mix with enough water and the vanilla extract to form a soft, but not too runny, frosting.

5 Drizzle the frosting over the chocolate brownies and let set. Dust with chocolate powder.

cannoli

makes twenty

3 tbsp lemon juice

3 tbsp water

1 large egg

1¾ cups all-purpose flour

1 tbsp superfine sugar

1 tsp ground allspice

pinch of salt

2 tbsp butter, softened

corn oil, for deep-frying

1 small egg white, beaten lightly

confectioners' sugar

FILLING

3¼ cups ricotta cheese, drained

4 tbsp confectioners' sugar

1 tsp vanilla extract

finely grated rind of 1 large orange

4 tbsp very finely chopped candied
    peel

1¾ oz/50 g semisweet chocolate,
    grated

pinch of ground cinnamon

2 tbsp Marsala wine or orange juice

1 Combine the lemon juice, water, and egg. Put the flour, sugar, spice, and salt into a food processor and quickly process. Add the butter, then, with the motor running, pour the egg mixture through the feed tube. Process until the mixture just forms a dough.

2 Turn the dough out onto a lightly floured counter and knead lightly. Wrap and let chill for at least 1 hour.

3 Meanwhile, make the filling. Beat the ricotta cheese until smooth. Sift in the confectioners' sugar, then beat in the remaining ingredients. Cover and let chill until required.

4 Roll out the dough on a floured counter until ⅟₁₆-inch/1.5-mm thick. Using a ruler, cut out 3 ½ x 3-inch/ 9 x 7.5-cm pieces, re-rolling and cutting the trimmings. The dough should make about 20 pieces.

5 Heat 2 inches/5 cm of oil in a skillet to 375°F/190°C. Roll a piece of dough around a greased cannoli mold, to just overlap the edge. Seal with egg white, pressing firmly.

Repeat with all the molds you have. Deep-fry 2 or 3 molds until the cannoli are golden, crisp, and bubbly.

6 Remove with a slotted spoon and drain on paper towels. Let cool, then carefully slide off the molds. Repeat with the remaining cannoli.

7 Store the cannoli unfilled in an airtight container for up to 2 days. Pipe in the filling no more than 30 minutes before serving to prevent the cannoli becoming soggy. Sift confectioners' sugar over the top just before serving.

chocolate & coconut cookies

makes twenty four

½ cup soft margarine

1 tsp vanilla extract

½ cup confectioners' sugar, sifted

1 cup all-purpose flour

2 tbsp unsweetened cocoa

⅔ cup shredded coconut

2 tbsp butter

3½ oz/100 g white marshmallows

⅓ cup shredded coconut

a little white chocolate, grated

1 Lightly grease a cookie sheet. Beat the margarine, vanilla extract, and confectioners' sugar together in a mixing bowl until fluffy. Sift the flour and cocoa together and beat it into the mixture with the coconut.

2 Roll rounded teaspoons of the mixture into balls and place on the prepared cookie sheet, allowing room for the cookies to spread during cooking.

3 Flatten the balls slightly and bake in a preheated oven, 350°F/ 180°C, for about 12–15 minutes, until just firm. Remove the cookies from the oven.

4 Let the chocolate and coconut cookies cool on the cookie sheet for a few minutes before carefully transferring to a wire rack. Let the cookies cool completely.

5 To make the frosting, place the butter and marshmallows in a small pan and heat gently, stirring until melted. Spread a little of the marshmallow frosting mixture over each cookie, using a knife or small spoon, and dip in the coconut. Let them set. Decorate the chocolate and coconut cookies with grated white chocolate before serving.

dutch macaroons

makes twenty

rice paper

2 egg whites

1 cup superfine sugar

1⅔ cups ground almonds

8 oz/225 g semisweet chocolate

COOK'S TIP

Rice paper is edible so you can just break off the excess from around the edge of the cookies. Remove it completely before dipping in the chocolate, if you prefer.

1 Cover 2 cookie sheets with rice paper. Whisk the egg whites in a large mixing bowl until stiff, then fold in the sugar and ground almonds.

2 Place the mixture in a large pastry bag fitted with a ½-inch/1-cm plain tip and pipe fingers, about 3-inches/7.5 cm-long, allowing space between them for the mixture to spread during cooking.

3 Bake in a preheated oven, 350°F/180°C, for 15–20 minutes, until golden. Transfer to a wire rack and let cool. Remove the excess rice paper from around the edges.

4 Melt the semisweet chocolate and dip the bottom of each cookie into the chocolate. Place the macaroons on a sheet of baking parchment and let set.

5 Drizzle any remaining chocolate over the top of the cookies (you may need to re-heat the chocolate in order to do this). Let the chocolate set before serving.

chocolate chip flapjacks

makes twelve

½ cup butter

⅓ cup superfine sugar

1 tbsp light corn syrup

4 cups rolled oats

½ cup semisweet chocolate chips

⅓ cup golden raisins

COOK'S TIP

The flapjacks will keep in
an airtight container for up
to 1 week, but they are so
delicious they are unlikely
to last that long!

1 Lightly grease a shallow
8-inch/20-cm square cake pan.

2 Place the butter, superfine sugar,
and light corn syrup in a pan and
cook over low heat, stirring until the
butter and sugar melt and the mixture
is well combined.

3 Remove the pan from the heat
and stir in the rolled oats until
they are well coated. Add the
chocolate chips and the golden raisins
and mix well.

4 Turn into the prepared pan and
press down well.

5 Bake in a preheated oven,
350°F/180°C, for 30 minutes. Let
cool slightly, then mark into fingers.
When the mixture is almost cold cut
into bars or squares and transfer to a
wire rack until cold.

chocolate chip cookies

makes eighteen

1½ cups all-purpose flour

1 tsp baking powder

½ cup soft margarine

scant ⅔ cup brown sugar

¼ cup superfine sugar

½ tsp vanilla extract

1 egg

⅔ cup semisweet chocolate chips

VARIATION

For Choc & Nut Cookies,
add ½ cup chopped hazelnuts
to the basic mixture.
For Double Choc Cookies,
beat in 1½ oz/40 g melted
semisweet chocolate.
For White Chocolate Chip
Cookies, use white chocolate
chips instead of the semisweet
chocolate chips.

1 Place all of the ingredients in a large mixing bowl and beat until they are thoroughly combined.

2 Lightly grease 2 cookie sheets. Place tablespoonfuls of the mixture onto the cookie sheets, spacing them well apart to allow for spreading during cooking.

3 Bake in a preheated oven, 375°F/190°C, for 10–12 minutes or until the cookies are golden brown.

4 Using a spatula, carefully transfer the chocolate chip cookies to a wire rack to cool completely.

millionaire's shortbread

serves four

1½ cups all-purpose flour

½ cup butter, cut into small pieces

⅓ cup brown sugar, sifted

TOPPING

4 tbsp butter

⅓ cup brown sugar

1¾ cups canned condensed milk

5½ oz/150 g light chocolate

1 Grease a 9-inch/23-cm square cake pan.

2 Sift the flour into a mixing bowl and rub in the butter with your fingertips until the mixture resembles fine bread crumbs. Add the sugar and mix to form a firm dough.

3 Press the dough into the bottom of the prepared pan and prick the bottom with a fork.

4 Bake in a preheated oven, 375°F/190°C, for 20 minutes, until lightly golden. Let cool in the pan.

5 To make the topping, place the butter, sugar, and condensed milk in a non-stick pan and cook over gentle heat, stirring constantly with a wooden spoon, until the mixture comes to a boil.

COOK'S TIP

Ensure the caramel layer is completely cool and set before coating it with the melted chocolate, otherwise they will mix together.

6 Lower the heat and cook for 4–5 minutes, until the caramel is pale golden and thick and is coming away from the sides of the pan. Pour the topping evenly over the shortbread layer and let cool.

7 When the caramel topping is firm, melt the light chocolate in a heatproof bowl set over a pan of simmering water. Spread the melted chocolate over the topping, let set in a cool place, then cut the shortbread into squares or fingers.

florentines

makes ten

4 tbsp butter

¼ cup superfine sugar

scant ¼ cup all-purpose flour, sifted

⅓ cup almonds, chopped

⅓ cup chopped candied peel

¼ cup raisins, chopped

2 tbsp chopped candied cherries

finely grated rind of ½ lemon

4½ oz/125 g semisweet chocolate,
   melted

VARIATION

Replace the semisweet chocolate
with white chocolate or, for a
dramatic effect, cover half of
the florentines in semisweet
chocolate and half in white.

1 Line 2 large cookie sheets with
baking parchment.

2 Heat the butter and superfine
sugar together in a small pan
until the butter has just melted and the
sugar dissolved. Remove the pan from
the heat.

3 Stir in the flour and mix well. Stir
in the chopped almonds, candied
peel, raisins, cherries, and lemon rind.
Place teaspoonfuls of the mixture well
apart on the cookie sheets.

4 Bake in a preheated oven,
350°F/180°C, for 10 minutes or
until they are lightly golden.

5 As soon as the florentines are
removed from the oven, press the
edges into neat shapes while still on
the cookie sheets, using a cookie
cutter. Let cool on the cookie sheets
until firm, then transfer to a wire rack
to cool completely.

6 Spread the melted chocolate
over the smooth side of each
florentine. As the chocolate starts to
set, mark wavy lines in it with a fork.
Let set, chocolate-side up.

lemon chocolate pinwheels

makes forty

¾ cup butter, softened

1⅓ cups superfine sugar

1 egg, beaten

3 cups all-purpose flour

1 oz/25 g semisweet chocolate,
   melted and cooled slightly

grated rind of 1 lemon

COOK'S TIP

To make rolling out easier, place
each piece of dough between
2 sheets of baking parchment.

1 Grease and flour several cookie
   sheets, enough to accommodate
40 cookies comfortably.

2 Cream the butter and sugar
   together in a large mixing bowl
until light and fluffy.

3 Gradually add the beaten egg to
   the creamed mixture, beating well
after each addition.

4 Sift the flour into the creamed
   mixture and mix thoroughly until
a soft dough forms.

5 Transfer half of the dough to
   another bowl and then beat in
the cooled melted chocolate.

6 Stir the grated lemon rind into the
   other half of the plain dough until
well incorporated.

7 Roll out the 2 pieces of dough on
   a lightly floured surface to form
rectangles of the same size.

8 Lay the lemon dough on top of
   the chocolate dough. Roll up the
dough tightly into a sausage shape,
using a sheet of baking parchment to
guide you. Let the dough chill in the
refrigerator to firm up.

9 Cut the roll into about 40 slices,
   place them on the cookie sheets,
and bake in a preheated oven, 375°F/
190°C, for 10–12 minutes or until the
slices are lightly golden. Transfer the
lemon chocolate pinwheels to a wire
rack and let them cool completely
before serving.

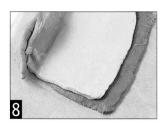

chocolate pretzels

makes thirty

generous ⅓ cup unsalted butter

½ cup superfine sugar

1 egg

2 cups all-purpose flour

¼ cup unsweetened cocoa

TO FINISH

1 tbsp butter

3½ oz/100 g semisweet chocolate

confectioners' sugar, for dusting

1 Lightly grease a cookie sheet with a little butter. Beat the butter and sugar together in a large mixing bowl until light and fluffy. Beat in the egg, ensuring all the ingredients are well combined.

2 Sift the flour and cocoa together and gradually beat into the egg mixture to form a soft dough. Use your fingers to incorporate the last of the flour and bring the dough together. Let chill for 15 minutes.

3 Break pieces from the dough and roll into thin sausage shapes about 4-inches/10-cm long and ¼-inch/6-mm thick. Carefully twist into pretzel shapes by making a circle, then twist the ends through each other to form a letter "B."

4 Place the chocolate pretzels on the prepared cookie sheet, slightly spaced apart to allow for spreading during cooking.

5 Bake in a preheated oven, 375°F/190°C, for 8–12 minutes. Let the pretzels cool slightly on the cookie sheet, then transfer them to a wire rack to cool completely.

6 Melt the butter and chocolate in a bowl set over a pan of gently simmering water, stirring to combine.

7 Dip half of each pretzel into the chocolate and allow the excess chocolate to drip back into the bowl. Place the pretzels on a sheet of baking parchment and let set.

8 When set, dust the non-chocolate-coated side of each pretzel with confectioners' sugar.

chocolate boxes

serves six

8 oz/225 g semisweet chocolate

about 8 oz/225 g bought or
    ready-made semisweet or
    chocolate sponge cake

2 tbsp apricot jelly

⅔ cup heavy cream

1 tbsp maple syrup

3½ oz/100 g prepared fresh fruit,
    such as small strawberries,
    raspberries, kiwifruit or red
    currants

1 Melt the semisweet chocolate and spread it evenly over a large sheet of baking parchment. Let the chocolate harden in a cool room.

2 When just set, cut the chocolate into 2-inch/5-cm squares and remove from the parchment. Make sure that your hands are as cool as possible and handle the chocolate as little as possible.

3 Cut the cake into 2 cubes, 2 inches/5 cm across, then cut each cube in half. Warm the apricot jelly in a small pan and brush it over the sides of the cake cubes. Carefully press a chocolate square on to each side of the cake cubes to make 4 chocolate boxes with cake at the bottom. Let chill in the refrigerator for 20 minutes.

4 Whip the cream with the maple syrup until just holding its shape. Spoon or pipe a little of the mixture into each chocolate box.

5 Decorate the top of each box with the prepared fruit. If wished, the fruit can be partially dipped into melted chocolate and allowed to harden before being placed into the boxes.

fried chocolate fingers

makes twenty four

4 eggs, beaten lightly

2½ cups milk

5 tbsp sherry

8 slices of day-old white bread,
½ inch/1 cm thick

4 tbsp corn oil

generous ½ cup superfine sugar

8 oz/225 g semisweet chocolate

vanilla ice cream, to serve (optional)

1 Pour the beaten eggs, milk, and sherry into a shallow dish and beat lightly to mix. Cut each slice of bread lengthwise into 3 fingers. Soak the bread fingers in the egg mixture until they are soft, then drain them on paper towels.

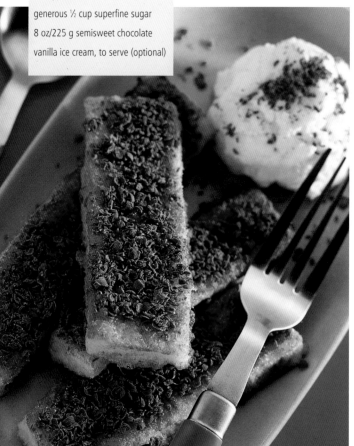

2 Heat the oil in a large, heavy-based skillet. Carefully add the bread fingers to the pan, in batches, and cook over medium heat for 12 minutes on each side, until golden. Using tongs, transfer the fingers to paper towels to drain.

3 When all the fingers are cooked and thoroughly drained, roll them first in the sugar and then in the grated chocolate. Pile on a warmed serving plate and serve immediately, with vanilla ice cream, if desired.

meringue fingers

makes thirty

1 egg white

¼ cup superfine sugar

1½ tsp unsweetened cocoa

5 oz/140 g semisweet chocolate,
   broken into pieces

1 Line a cookie sheet with baking parchment. Whisk the egg white until it forms soft peaks. Whisk in half the sugar and continue whisking until stiff and glossy. Fold in the remaining sugar and the cocoa.

2 Spoon the mixture into a pastry bag fitted with a ½-inch/1-cm round tip. Pipe fingers about 3-inches/7.5-cm long onto the prepared cookie sheet, spacing them at least 1-inch/2.5-cm apart. Bake in apreheated oven, 250ºF/120ºC for 1 hour, until completely dry. Remove from the oven and transfer to a wire rack to cool.

3 Put the chocolate into the top of a double boiler or in a heatproof bowl set over a pan of barely

simmering water. Heat, stirring constantly, until the chocolate has melted and the mixture is smooth. Remove from the heat. Cool slightly, then dip the meringue fingers into the mixture, one at a time, to half-coat them. You can either coat one end completely, leaving the other plain, or dip the fingers at an angle so half the length is coated. Place the fingers on baking parchment to set.

Candy & Drinks

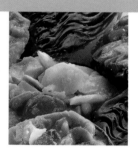

There is nothing quite as nice as home-made chocolates and candy—they leave the average box of chocolates in the shade! You'll find recipes in this chapter to suit everybody's taste. Wonderful, rich, melt-in-the-mouth Italian Chocolate Truffles, Chocolate Marzipans, Nutty Chocolate Clusters, Mini Chocolate Tartlets, and rich Liqueur Chocolates—they're all here. There is even some Easy Chocolate Fudge, so there is no need to fiddle about with sugar thermometers.

Looking for something to wash it all down? We have included delightfully cool summer chocolate drinks and, for warmth and comfort on winter nights, hot drinks that will simply put instant hot chocolate to shame. Enjoy!

liqueur chocolates

makes forty

3½ oz/100 g semisweet chocolate

about 5 candied cherries, halved

about 10 hazelnuts or macadamia
    nuts

⅔ cup heavy cream

2 tbsp confectioners' sugar

4 tbsp liqueur

TO FINISH

1¾ oz/50 g semisweet chocolate,
    melted

a little white chocolate, melted, or
    white chocolate curls (see
    page 7), or extra nuts and cherries

COOK'S TIP

Candy cases can vary in size.
Use the smallest you can find
for this recipe.

---

1 Line a cookie sheet with a sheet of baking parchment. Break the semisweet chocolate into pieces, place in a bowl and set over a pan of hot water. Stir until melted. Spoon the chocolate into 20 paper candy cases, spreading up the sides with a small spoon or brush. Place upside down on the cookie sheet and let set.

2 Carefully peel away the paper cases. Place a cherry or nut in the bottom of each cup.

3 To make the filling, place the heavy cream in a mixing bowl and sift the confectioners' sugar on top. Whisk the cream until it is just holding its shape, then whisk in the liqueur to flavor it.

4 Place the cream in a pastry bag fitted with a ½-inch/1-cm plain tip and pipe a little into each chocolate case. Let chill for 20 minutes.

5 To finish, spoon the semisweet chocolate over the cream to cover it and pipe the melted white chocolate on top, swirling it into the semisweet

chocolate with a toothpick. Let harden. Alternatively, cover the cream with the melted semisweet chocolate and decorate with white chocolate curls before setting. If you prefer, place a small piece of nut or cherry on top of the cream, then cover with semisweet chocolate.

nutty chocolate clusters

makes thirty

6 oz/175 g white chocolate

3½ oz/100 g graham crackers

⅔ cup chopped macadamia nuts or
brazil nuts

1 oz/25 g preserved ginger,
chopped (optional)

6 oz/175 g semisweet chocolate

1 Line a cookie sheet with a sheet
of baking parchment. Break the
white chocolate into small pieces and
melt in a large mixing bowl set over a
pan of gently simmering water.

2 Break the graham crackers into
small pieces. Stir the crackers into
the melted chocolate with the chopped
nuts and preserved ginger (if using).

3 Place heaping teaspoons of the
chocolate cluster mixture onto the
prepared cookie sheet.

4 Chill the chocolate cluster mixture
until set, then carefully remove
from the baking parchment.

5 Melt the semisweet chocolate and
let it cool slightly. Dip the clusters
into the chocolate, letting the excess to
drip back into the bowl. Return to the
cookie sheet and let chill until set.

fruit & nut fudge

makes twenty-five

9 oz/250 g semisweet chocolate

2 tbsp butter

4 tbsp canned evaporated milk

3 cups confectioners' sugar, sifted

½ cup coarsely chopped hazelnuts

⅓ cup golden raisins

VARIATION

Vary the nuts used in this recipe; try making the fudge with almonds, brazil nuts, walnuts, or pecans.

1 Lightly grease an 8-inch/20-cm square cake pan.

2 Break the chocolate into pieces and place it in a bowl with the butter and evaporated milk. Set the bowl over a pan of gently simmering water and stir until the chocolate and butter have melted and the ingredients are well combined.

3 Remove the bowl from the heat and gradually beat in the confectioners' sugar. Stir the hazelnuts and golden raisins into the mixture. Press the fudge into the prepared pan and smooth the top. Chill until firm.

4 Tip the fudge out onto a cutting board and cut into squares. Place in paper candy cases and let chill in the refrigerator until required.

mini chocolate tartlets

makes eighteen

1½ cups all-purpose flour

⅓ cup butter

1 tbsp superfine sugar

about 1 tbsp water

FILLING

3½ oz/100 g full-fat soft cheese

2 tbsp superfine sugar

1 small egg, beaten lightly

1¾ oz/50 g semisweet chocolate

TO DECORATE

generous ⅓ cup heavy cream

semisweet chocolate curls (see
    page 7)

unsweetened cocoa, for dusting

COOK'S TIP

The tartlets can be made up to
3 days ahead. Decorate on the
day of serving, preferably no
more than 4 hours in advance.

1 Sift the flour into a mixing bowl.
Cut the butter into small pieces
and rub in until the mixture resembles
fine bread crumbs. Stir in the sugar.
Add enough water to mix to a soft
dough, then cover with plastic wrap
and let chill for 15 minutes.

2 Roll out the dough on a lightly
floured counter and use to line 18
mini tartlet pans or mini muffin pans.
Prick the tartlet shells with a toothpick.

3 Beat the full-fat soft cheese and
the sugar together. Beat in the
egg. Melt the chocolate and beat it
into the mixture. Spoon into the tartlet
shells and bake in a preheated oven,
375°F/190°C, for 15 minutes, until the
dough is crisp and the soft cheese and
chocolate filling set. Place the pans on
a wire rack to cool completely.

4 Chill the tartlets. Whip the cream
until it is just holding its shape.
Place the cream in a pastry bag fitted
with a star tip and pipe rosettes of
whipped cream on top of the chocolate
tartlets. Decorate with chocolate curls
and finish with a dusting of cocoa.

rocky road bites

makes eighteen

FILLING

4½ oz/125 g light chocolate

2½ oz/50 g mini multi-colored
marshmallows

¼ cup chopped walnuts

1 oz/25 g no-soak dried apricots,
chopped

VARIATION

If you cannot find mini
marshmallows, use large
ones and chop them before
mixing them into the
melted chocolate.

1 Line a cookie sheet with baking parchment and set aside.

2 Break the chocolate into small pieces and place in a large mixing bowl. Set the bowl over a pan of simmering water and stir until the chocolate has melted.

3 Stir in the marshmallows, walnuts, and apricots, and toss in the melted chocolate until well covered.

4 Place heaping teaspoons of the marshmallow mixture onto the prepared cookie sheet.

5 Let chill in the refrigerator until the candy is set.

6 Once they are set, carefully remove the rocky road bites from the baking parchment.

7 Place in paper candy cases to serve, if wished.

232

chocolate mascarpone cups

makes twenty

3½ oz/100 g semisweet chocolate

FILLING

3½ oz/100 g light or semisweet
chocolate

¼ tsp vanilla extract

7 oz/200 g mascarpone cheese

unsweetened cocoa, for dusting

VARIATION

Mascarpone is a rich Italian
soft cheese made from fresh
cream, so it has a high fat
content. Its delicate flavor
blends well with chocolate.

1 Line a cookie sheet with a sheet of baking parchment. Break the semisweet chocolate into pieces, place in a bowl and set over a pan of hot water. Stir until melted. Spoon the chocolate into 20 paper candy cases, spreading up the sides with a small spoon or brush. Place the chocolate cups upside down on the cookie sheet and let set.

2 When set, carefully peel away the paper cases.

3 To make the filling, melt the chocolate. Place the mascarpone cheese in a bowl and beat in the vanilla extract and melted chocolate until well combined. Let the mixture chill in the refrigerator, beating occasionally until firm enough to pipe.

4 Place the mascarpone filling in a pastry bag fitted with a star tip and pipe the mixture into the cups. Decorate with a dusting of cocoa.

rum truffles

makes twenty

5½ oz/125 g semisweet chocolate

small piece of butter

2 tbsp rum

½ cup shredded coconut

3½ oz/100 g cake crumbs

6 tbsp confectioners' sugar

2 tbsp unsweetened cocoa

COOK'S TIP

Make sure the chocolate is cut into even sized pieces. This way, you will ensure that it all melts at the same rate.

1 Break the chocolate into pieces and place in a bowl with the butter. Set the bowl over a pan of gently simmering water, stir until melted and combined.

2 Remove from the heat and beat in the rum. Stir in the shredded coconut, cake crumbs, and two-thirds of the confectioners' sugar. Beat until combined. Add a little extra rum if the mixture is stiff.

3 Roll the mixture into small balls and place them on a sheet of baking parchment. Chill until firm.

4 Strain the remaining confectioners' sugar onto a large plate. Sift the cocoa onto another plate. Roll half of the truffles in the confectioners' sugar until thoroughly coated and roll the remaining rum truffles in the cocoa.

5 Place the truffles in paper candy cases and let chill in the refrigerator until required.

VARIATION

Make the truffles with white chocolate and replace the rum with coconut-flavored liqueur or milk. Roll them in unsweetened cocoa or dip in melted light chocolate.

mini chocolate cones

makes ten

2¾ oz/75 g semisweet chocolate

generous ⅓ cup heavy cream

1 tbsp confectioners' sugar

1 tbsp crème de menthe

chocolate-coated coffee beans, to

decorate (optional)

1 Cut 10 circles, 3 inches/7.5 cm across, out of baking parchment. Shape each circle into a cone shape and secure with sticky tape.

2 Break the chocolate into pieces, place in a bowl and set over a pan of hot water. Stir until melted. Using a small brush, coat the inside of each cone with the melted chocolate.

3 Brush a second layer of chocolate on the inside of the cones and let chill until set. Carefully peel away the baking parchment.

4 Place the cream, confectioners' sugar, and crème de menthe in a mixing bowl and whip until just holding its shape. Place the flavored cream in a pastry bag fitted with a star tip and carefully pipe the mixture into the chocolate cones.

5 Decorate the filled mini chocolate cones with chocolate-coated coffee beans (if using) and let chill in the refrigerator until required.

collettes

makes twenty

3½ oz/100 g white chocolate

FILLING

5½ oz/150 g orange-flavored
    semisweet chocolate

⅔ cup heavy cream

2 tbsp confectioners' sugar

COOK'S TIP

If they do not hold their
shape well, use 2 cases to make
a double thickness mold. Foil
cases are firmer, so use these if
you can find them.

1 Line a cookie sheet with baking parchment. Break the white chocolate into pieces, place in a bowl, and set over a pan of hot water. Stir until melted. Spoon the melted chocolate into 20 paper candy cases, spreading up the sides with a small spoon or brush. Place upside down on the prepared cookie sheet and let set.

2 When the chocolate has set, peel away the paper cases.

3 To make the filling, melt the orange-flavored chocolate and place in a mixing bowl with the heavy cream and the confectioners' sugar. Beat until smooth. Chill until the mixture becomes firm enough to pipe, stirring occasionally.

4 Place the filling in a pastry bag fitted with a star tip and pipe a little into each candy case. Chill the collettes until required.

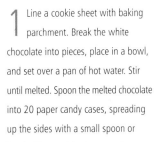

237

chocolate marzipans

makes thirty

1 lb/450 g marzipan

⅓ cup very finely chopped candied cherries

1 oz/25 g preserved ginger, chopped very finely

1¾ oz/50 g no-soak dried apricots, very finely chopped 12 oz/350 g semisweet chocolate

1 oz/25 g white chocolate

confectioners' sugar, to dust

1 Line a cookie sheet with baking parchment. Divide the marzipan into 3 balls and knead each ball to soften it.

2 Work the candied cherries into one portion of the marzipan by kneading on a counter lightly dusted with confectioners' sugar.

3 Do the same with the preserved ginger and another portion of marzipan, and then the apricots and the third portion of marzipan.

4 Form each flavored portion of marzipan into small balls, keeping the different flavors separate.

5 Break the semisweet chocolate into pieces, place in a bowl, and set over a pan of hot water. Stir until melted. Dip one of each flavored ball of marzipan into the chocolate by spiking each one with a toothpick, letting the excess chocolate to drip back into the bowl.

6 Place the balls in clusters made up of the 3 flavors on the cookie sheet. Repeat with the remaining marzipan balls. Chill until set.

7 Melt the white chocolate and drizzle a little over the tops of each cluster of marzipan balls. Chill until hardened, then remove from the baking parchment and dust the marzipan with sugar to serve.

VARIATION

Coat the marzipan balls in white or light chocolate and drizzle with semisweet chocolate, if you prefer.

mini florentines

makes forty

⅓ cup butter

⅓ cup superfine sugar

2 tbsp golden raisins or raisins

2 tbsp chopped candied cherries

2 tbsp chopped candied ginger

1 oz/25 g sunflower seeds

¾ cup slivered almonds

2 tbsp heavy cream

6 oz/175 g semisweet chocolate

1 Grease and flour 2 cookie sheets or line with baking parchment.

2 Place the butter in a small pan and heat gently until melted. Add the sugar, stir until dissolved, then bring the mixture to a boil. Remove from the heat and stir in the golden raisins or raisins, cherries, ginger, sunflower seeds, and almonds. Mix well, then beat in the cream.

3 Place small teaspoons of the fruit and nut mixture onto the prepared cookie sheet, allowing plenty of space for the mixture to spread. Bake in a preheated oven, at 350°F/180°C, for 10–12 minutes or until light golden in color.

4 Remove from the oven and, while still hot, use a circular cookie cutter to pull in the edges to form perfect circles. Let cool and go crisp before removing from the cookie sheet.

5 Break the chocolate into pieces, place in a bowl over a pan of hot water, and stir until melted. Spread most of the chocolate onto a sheet of baking parchment. When the chocolate is on the point of setting, carefully place the cookies flat-side down on the chocolate and let harden completely.

6 Cut around the florentines and remove from the baking parchment. Spread a little more chocolate on the coated side of the florentines and use a fork to mark waves in the chocolate. Let set. Arrange the florentines on a plate (or in a presentation box for a gift) with alternate sides facing upward. Keep the florentines cool.

easy chocolate fudge

makes twenty-five pieces

1 lb 2 oz/500 g semisweet
　chocolate
⅓ cup unsalted butter
1¾ cups canned condensed milk
½ tsp vanilla extract

1 Lightly grease an 8-inch/20-cm square cake pan.

2 Break the chocolate into pieces and place in a large pan with the butter and condensed milk.

3 Heat gently, stirring until the chocolate and butter melts and the mixture is smooth. Do not let the mixture boil.

4 Remove from the heat. Beat in the vanilla extract, then beat the mixture for a few minutes until thickened. Pour it into the prepared pan and smooth the top.

5 Chill the mixture in the refrigerator until firm.

6 Tip the fudge out onto a large cutting board and cut into squares to serve.

COOK'S TIP

Store the fudge in an airtight container in a cool, dry place for up to 1 month. Do not freeze.

chocolate cherries

makes twenty-four

12 candied cherries

2 tbsp rum or brandy

9 oz/250 g marzipan

5½ oz/125 g semisweet chocolate

extra light, semisweet, or white
chocolate, to decorate (optional)

VARIATION

Flatten the marzipan and use it
to mold around the cherries to
cover them, then dip in the
chocolate as in main recipe.

1 Line a cookie sheet with a sheet of baking parchment.

2 Cut the candied cherries in half and place in a small bowl. Add the rum or brandy and stir to coat. Let the cherries soak for at least 1 hour, stirring occasionally.

3 Divide the marzipan into 24 pieces and roll each piece into a ball. Press half a cherry into the top of each marzipan ball.

4 Break the chocolate into pieces, place in a bowl, and set over a pan of hot water. Stir until melted.

5 Dip each candy into the melted chocolate using a toothpick, allowing the excess to drip back into the bowl. Place the coated cherries on the baking parchment and chill until set.

6 If wished, melt a little extra chocolate and drizzle it over the top of the coated cherries. Let set.

cocochoc pyramids

makes twelve

⅔ cup water

2¼ cups granulated sugar

pinch of cream of tartar

generous 1 cup shredded coconut

1 tbsp heavy cream

few drops of yellow liquid food
   coloring

3 oz/85 g semisweet chocolate,
   broken into pieces

COOK'S TIP

For the best results when
cooking with chocolate, always
try to use the best quality
chocolate that you can find.

1 Pour the water into a heavy-based pan, add the sugar, and stir over low heat until the sugar has dissolved. Stir in a pinch of cream of tartar and bring to a boil. Boil steadily, without stirring, until the temperature reaches 238°F/119°C on a sugar thermometer. If you do not have a sugar thermometer, test the syrup frequently by dropping a small quantity into a bowl of cold water. If the mixture can then be rolled between your finger and thumb to make a soft ball, it is ready.

2 Remove the pan from the heat and beat in the coconut and cream. Continue to beat for 5–10 minutes, until the mixture becomes cloudy. Beat in a few drops of yellow food coloring, then let cool. When cool enough to handle, take small pieces of the mixture and form them into pyramids. Place the pyramids on a sheet of baking parchment and let harden.

3 Put the chocolate into the top of a double boiler or in a heatproof bowl set over a pan of barely simmering water. Stir over low heat until melted, then remove from the heat. Dip the bottom of the pyramids into the melted chocolate and let set.

italian chocolate truffles

makes twenty four

6 oz/175 g semisweet chocolate

2 tbsp Amaretto liqueur or orange-
  flavored liqueur

3 tbsp unsalted butter

4 tbsp confectioners' sugar

½ cup ground almonds

1¾ oz/50 g grated chocolate

VARIATION

The almond-flavored liqueur
gives these truffles an authentic
Italian flavor. The original almond
liqueur, Amaretto di Saronno,
comes from Saronno in Italy.

1 Melt the semisweet chocolate with the liqueur in a bowl set over a pan of hot water, stirring until well combined.

2 Add the butter and stir until it has melted. Stir in the confectioners' sugar and the ground almonds.

3 Let the mixture stand in a cool place until it is firm enough to roll into 24 balls.

4 Place the grated chocolate on a plate and roll the truffles in the chocolate to coat them.

5 Place the truffles in paper candy cases and let chill.

white chocolate truffles

makes twenty

2 tbsp unsalted butter

5 tbsp heavy cream

8 oz/225 g good-quality Swiss
   white chocolate

1 tbsp orange-flavored liqueur,
   optional

TO FINISH

3½ oz/100 g white chocolate

1 Line a jelly roll pan with a sheet of baking parchment.

2 Place the butter and cream in a small pan and bring slowly to a boil, stirring constantly. Boil the mixture for 1 minute, then remove the pan from the heat.

3 Break the chocolate into pieces and add to the cream. Stir until melted, then beat in the orange-flavored liqueur (if using).

4 Pour into the prepared pan and chill for about 2 hours, until firm.

5 Break off pieces of the truffle mixture and roll them into balls. Chill for another 30 minutes before finishing the truffles.

6 To finish, melt the white chocolate in a bowl set over a pan of gently simmering water. Dip the balls in the chocolate, allowing the excess to drip back into the bowl. Place on non-stick baking parchment, swirl the chocolate with the tines of a fork, and let harden.

7 For an effective decoration, and a pleasing color contrast, drizzle a little melted semisweet chocolate over the truffles if wished and then let them set before serving.

4

5

6

candied citrus peel

makes sixty

1 large unwaxed, thick-skinned
  orange
1 large unwaxed, thick-skinned
  lemon
1 large unwaxed, thick-skinned lime
3 cups superfine sugar
1¼ cups water
4½ oz/125 g best-quality semisweet
  chocolate, chopped (optional)

1 Cut the orange into fourths lengthwise and squeeze the juice into a cup to drink, or to use in another recipe. Cut each fourth in half lengthwise to make 8 pieces.

2 Cut the fruit and pith away from the rind. If any of the pith remains on the rind, lay the knife almost flat on the white side of the rind and gently "saw" backward and forward to slice it off because it will taste bitter.

3 Repeat with the lemon and lime, only cutting the lime into quarters. Cut each piece into 3 or 4 thin strips to make 60–80 strips in total. Place the strips in a pan of water and boil for 30 seconds. Drain the strips thoroughly.

4 Dissolve the sugar in the water in a pan over medium heat, stirring. Increase the heat and bring to a boil, without stirring. When the syrup becomes clear, turn the heat to its lowest setting.

5 Add the citrus strips, using a wooden spoon to push them in without stirring simmer in the syrup for 30 minutes, without stirring. Turn off the heat and set aside for at least 6 hours, until completely cool.

6 Line a cookie sheet with foil. Skim off the thin crust on top of the syrup without stirring. Remove the rind strips, one by one, from the syrup, shaking off any excess. Place on the foil to cool.

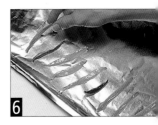

7 If you want to dip the candied peel in chocolate, melt the chocolate. Working with one piece of candied peel at a time, dip the peel halfway into the chocolate. Return to the foil and let set. Store in an airtight container.

chocolate eggnog

serves four

8 egg yolks

1 cup sugar

4 cups milk

8 oz/225 g semisweet chocolate

⅔ cup dark rum

1 Beat the egg yolks with the sugar until thickened.

2 Pour the milk into a large pan. Grate the chocolate and add it to the milk. Bring to a boil, then remove from the heat and gradually beat in the egg yolk mixture. Stir in the rum and pour into heatproof glasses.

hot brandy chocolate

serves four

4 cups milk

4 oz/115 g semisweet chocolate,
   broken into pieces

2 tbsp sugar

5 tbsp brandy

TO DECORATE

5 tbsp whipped cream

4 tsp unsweetened cocoa, sifted

Pour the milk into a pan and
bring to a boil, then remove from
the heat. Place the chocolate in a small
pan and add 2 tablespoons of the
hot milk. Stir over low heat until
the chocolate has melted. Stir the
chocolate mixture into the remaining
milk and add the sugar.

Stir in the brandy and pour into
4 heatproof glasses. Top each
with a swirl of whipped cream and
sprinkle with a little sifted cocoa.

cold chocolate drinks

serves two

CHOCOLATE MILK SHAKE

2 cups ice-cold milk

3 tbsp drinking chocolate powder

3 scoops chocolate ice cream

unsweetened cocoa, for dusting

CHOCOLATE ICE CREAM SODA

5 tbsp Glossy Chocolate Sauce (see
   page 104)

soda water

2 scoops chocolate ice cream

heavy cream, whipped

semisweet or light chocolate, grated

1 To make the chocolate milk shake,
pour half of the ice-cold milk in
a blender.

2 Add the drinking chocolate
powder to the blender and
1 scoop of the chocolate ice cream.
Blend until frothy and well mixed.
Stir in the remaining milk.

3 Place the remaining 2 scoops of
chocolate ice cream in 2 tall
serving glasses and carefully pour the
chocolate milk over the ice scoops of
chocolate cream.

4 Sprinkle a little cocoa over the
top of each drink and serve
immediately.

5 To make the chocolate ice cream
soda, divide the Glossy Chocolate
Sauce between 2 glasses.

6 Add a little soda water to each
glass and stir to combine the
sauce and soda water. Place a scoop
of ice cream in each glass and top up
with more of the soda water.

7 Place a dollop of whipped heavy
cream on the top, if liked, and
sprinkle with a little grated semisweet
or light chocolate.

COOK'S TIP

Served in a tall glass, a
milk shake or an ice cream
soda makes a delicious
snack in a drink. Serve with
straws, if wished.